Co-operatives that Work

Co-operatives that Work
New Constitutions, Conversions and Tax

by Paddy Smith LL.B.
retired Solicitor

Rules and Memorandum and Articles
by David Chivers B.A. (Cantab.)
of Lincoln's Inn, Barrister

Employee Trust Settlements
by Giles Goodfellow M.A. (Cantab.) LL.M. (U Va. Law School).
of Middle Temple, Barrister

SPOKESMAN

First published in 1988 by:
Spokesman
Bertrand Russell House
Gamble Street
Nottingham, England
Tel. 0602 708318

Copyright © Paddy Smith and David Chivers

This book is copyright under the Berne Convention. All rights are reserved. Apart from any fair dealing for the purpose of private study, research, criticism or review, as permitted under the Copyright Act, 1956, no part of this publication may be reproduced, stored in a retrieval system, or transmitted, in any form or by any means, electronic, electrical, chemical, mechanical, photocopying, recording or otherwise, without the prior permission of the copyright owner. Enquiries should be addressed to the publishers.

British Library Cataloguing in Publication Data
Smith, P. Co-operatives that work: new constitutions, conversions, and tax.
 1. Producer co-operatives — Great Britain
 I. Title
 334'.6'0941 HD3175.A4

ISBN 0-85124-452-1
ISBN 0-85124-462-9 Pbk

Printed by the Russell Press Ltd, Nottingham
(Tel. 0602 784505)

Contents

Preface	9
Introduction	**11**
Existing Constitutions	11
New Models	13
Different Economic Ideologies	13
Management and Accountability	14
Trade Union Roles	16
Slow Growth of Producer Co-operatives	17
Worker Buy-outs as possible Growth Area	18
Chapter 1: Some Existing Constitutions	**19**
Traditional Producer Co-operatives	19
Industrial and Provident Societies Acts	19
Producer Co-operatives	22
Conflicting Interests of Employee and Non-Employee Members	24
New Wave Co-operatives or Common Ownerships	25
Worker Controlled Businesses with Labour hiring Capital	25
ICOM Models	26
Mondragon Co-operatives and Job Ownership Ltd. (JOL)	28
Conventional Businesses	30
Partnerships	30
Company Limited by Shares	31
Chapter 2: New Model Constitutions	**35**
Members' Capital	35
Partnership as a Model	35
Members' Reserve Accounts	36
Share Capital and Loans	37

Co-operative Model	39
General Reserves	39
Capitalising General Reserves in an Employees' Trust	40
Members' Capital Contribution	43
Outside Finance	44
Short Term Finance	44
Longer Term Finance	44
A Type of Equity	45
Greater Need for External Finance	47
Management Structure	47
Legal Standing of Committee or Board	47
Accountability to Members	48
Electing Committee or Board by Proportional Representation	48

Chapter 3: Conversions and Take-Overs — 51

Purchase of an Existing Business	51
Available Choices	51
Redundancy Payments	51
Agreement to form a Worker-Controlled Firm	52
Purchase of a Conventional Company and Conversion to a Worker-Controlled Company	52
(a) Reorganisation of the Company	52
(b) Re-allocation of Shares	53
(c) Purchase by the Company of its own Shares	55
Purchase of a Conventional Company and Conversion to an Industrial and Provident Societies Act Society	57
Purchase of a Society and Conversion to a Worker-Controlled Society or Companies Act Company	59
Puchase of the Assets and Goodwill of the Existing Business	60
Sale of a Worker Controlled Firm and Conversion to a Conventional Company	61

Chapter 4: Gift of a Conventional Company to the Employees — 63

Inheritance Tax Exemption and Capital Gains Tax Roll-Over Relief	63
The Period and Terms of the Trust	66

Chapter 5: Income and Corporation Tax 71

Corporation Tax 71
Members' Loan Accounts and Members'
Reserve Accounts 72
Lump Sum Payments and Pensions on Retirement 72
Profit Sharing Schemes 74
Close Companies 77
Relief for Interest on Money Borrowed 77
The Business Expansion Scheme 79

Model Forms or Precedents 81

Introduction to the Model Rules and
Memorandum and Articles of Association
of a Worker Controlled Co-operative 81
Rules of a Worker Controlled Co-operative Society 83
A Worker Controlled Private Company Limited
by Shares:
    Memorandum of Association 114
    Articles of Association 120
Employee Trust Settlement:
    I For Capitalising Reserves 132
    II As a Vehicle for a Gift of a Conventional
       Company to its Employees with Tax Relief 139

**Appendix: Table A of the Companies (Tables A to F)
Regulations 1985** 147

Preface

The 1970s and '80s have shown an upsurge of interest in industrial and service co-operatives pioneered by the Industrial Common Ownership Movement (ICOM). In 1978 the Government created the Co-operative Development Agency (CDA) which has given priority to the promotion of industrial and service co-operatives. Job Ownership Limited (JOL) was formed in 1978 as a non-profit making company to assist the ownership and control of industrial and service enterprises by the people who work in them. In the autumn of 1982 there were 59 local Co-operative Development Agencies listed by the CDA which have risen to about 80 four years later. In 1981 the Wales TUC published a study entitled *Co-operation and Job Creation in Wales: A Feasibility Study* and since then has set up a Resource Centre to assist the formation of worker co-operatives. Traditionally, producer co-operatives were registered under the Industrial and Provident Societies Acts (I & PS Acts) which provide a quite distinct legal framework for Societies from that provided by the Companies Acts for Companies. But the present promoters of worker controlled enterprises are not confining themselves to registration under the Industrial and Provident Societies Acts. ICOM and the CDA provide a model Memorandum and Articles of Association for registration as a Company Limited by Guarantee as well as I & PS Act Rules and JOL are experimenting with models for registration as a company limited by shares. The present drive seems to be to provide constitutions which guarantee control by the work-force regardless of the form of legal constitution. Also there is a search for stability as it is widely believed that the framework provided by the I & PS Acts, if unmodified, tends to produce pressure either to convert to a conventional company or to wind up in order to realise a capital gain once the society has accumulated substantial reserves.

Parallel to this growth in producer co-operatives has been a big increase in management buy-outs. They are sometimes referred to as worker buy-outs when all employees are encouraged to contribute to their purchase. On privatisation the question is frequently raised whether the employees should take over under some form of worker co-operative. If the new firm is constituted as a conventional company with shares then there is another problem over stability, this time of stability of control by the work-force as there is nothing to stop the purchase of a controlling interest by a few individuals.

We are attempting to tackle these problems from a lawyer's point of view rather than an ideological one. The only available model Rules for direct worker control are either of traditional co-operatives or ICOM common ownership societies. There are no readily available, flexible, general purpose model Rules for a worker-controlled producer co-operative which is not a common ownership and there is no model Memorandum and Articles of Association of a company limited by shares with built-in provisions for worker control. We have provided our version of both. We have attempted to show how existing legal provisions can be adapted to secure worker-control, how they fit into current taxation of companies and how a conventional company can be converted to one controlled by its work-force and vice versa.

We hope that this short book will be of use, not only to would-be co-operators, but also to solicitors and accountants who are called upon to advise them.

Note:
In view of fast moving developments in the law of taxation advice should be taken on the current position. Tax relief on Profit Related Pay contained in the Finance Act, 1987, is not considered in the text but might well be relevant.

Introduction

Existing Constitutions

Co-operative enterprises of one sort or another have been in existence for centuries[1]. Sometimes they take the form of partnerships but, of course, many partnerships are not worker-controlled but are two tier organisations with the partners co-operating amongst themselves and employing non-partners. In 1852 the first Industrial and Provident Societies Act (I & PS Act) was passed which provided for legal incorporation of co-operative societies and, since then, this has been regarded as the normal method of incorporating a worker-controlled business[2]. In fact, this and subsequent Acts do not provide for worker-control but for member-control on a one person one vote basis as opposed to control based on capital contribution, but members are not restricted to workers. The Acts further limit the domination of capital by providing that the rate of interest on capital has to be limited. The framework provided by the Acts has not proved satisfactory, in its unmodified form, for worker-controlled businesses and two major problems have emerged. The first is that over time non-employee members tend to exceed employee members so that the Society ceases to be worker-controlled[3]. The second is that with a limited return to capital and profits going to employee members, the non-employee members are tempted to convert to a conventional company or to sell the business in order to realise a capital gain. The capital gain arises because profits which are not distributed to employee members are ploughed back and on a distribution surplus assets, swelled by these ploughed back profits and appreciation in value of

---

1. For historical introduction see *Workers' Co-operatives, Jobs and Dreams* by Jenny Thornley, Heinemann Educational Books 1981; *The Case for Workers' Co-ops* by Robert Oakeshott, Routledge and Kegan Paul Ltd., 1978 and *The New Worker Co-operatives* edited by Ken Coates, Spokesman 1976.
2. See page 19 et seq.
3. See page 23.

capital assets, can go to the shareholders in proportion to their shares[4].

Producer co-operatives reached their peak in numbers in the 1890s when there were well over 100 in existence but have declined since and by 1973 there were apparently less than 25 with very few new Societies being formed under the traditional rules[5]. In 1958 the Industrial Common Ownership Movement (ICOM) was formed[6] which has pioneered what has been called the New Wave Co-operatives which have been forming rapidly since 1975[7] though they tend to be small. ICOM have provided model rules and a model memorandum and articles of association of a company limited by guarantee, in which they have tackled this problem of membership by providing that only employees may be members and on employment ceasing membership is terminated. This means that the business must remain worker-controlled and so there are no non-employee members to force a winding up and distribution of assets. However, ICOM have gone further and attempted to remove possible pressure from employee members to wind up by providing that on a winding up surplus assets shall not be distributed to members but shall go to another common ownership enterprise or central fund or to charity[8]. These two provisions as to membership and distribution of assets are what constitute a common ownership society as opposed to any other type of co-operative society. Job Ownership Ltd. (JOL) are producing a model based on a conventional company limited by shares with the majority of shares held by a trust under which substantial powers of control and right to profits are given to the employees. This is on the lines of the John Lewis Partnership Ltd. and Scott Bader Commonwealth Ltd[9]. The Co-operative Development Agency (CDA) have produced model rules for a traditional type of producer co-operative with an alternative memorandum and articles of association of a company limited by guarantee, which permits non-employee members. They have also issued a guide to the formation of an equity participating co-operative, registered as a company limited by guarantee, to hold some of the equity shares in a conventional company.

4. See page 24.
5. See page 22.
6. See page 25.
7. The CDA of Broadmead House, 21 Panton Street, London SW1Y 4DR, listed 330 in the Autumn of 1980, 495 (excluding Neighbourhood Co-operatives) in the Autumn of 1982, 911 in 1984 and 1476 in 1986.
8. See page 27.
9. See page 67.

New Models

What are missing are general purpose model constitutions which give direct worker control (not mediated through a trust or separate co-operative) but are not limited to common ownership enterprises. We have made a start by providing model Rules for registration under the I & PS Acts and a model memorandum and articles of association for registration under the Companies Acts[10]. They are designed to be ideology-free but, nevertheless, available for use by co-operators whatever their attitude or ideology. We have identified what appear to be the generally accepted requirements for a worker-controlled business[11], i.e. control by employee members on the basis of one person, one vote, membership open to all employees (with only limited exceptions) and capital paid no more than that required to obtain it. These principles we have written into the constitutions but otherwise have not tried to dictate how the employees shall exercise control apart from putting in normal administrative provisions and meeting statutory requirements. Every company or society has its own objectives and priorities and develops a normal way of doing things, which may be changed from time to time. These objectives and procedures may be informal or may be written down as subsidiary rules which can be changed without the formality and expense of changing the constitution. A variety of attitudes and ideologies were expressed at a conference on the Mondragon Co-operatives of Northern Spain organised by the Co-operative Research Unit (CRU) of the Open University in 1981, a report of which is published by the CRU under the title *Mondragon Co-operatives - Myth or Model*. A good deal of concern and difference in outlook were expressed over matters of finance, over the power of managers and over trade union involvement.

Different Economic Ideologies

There are a number of points of difference over finance. Some co-operators want equal pay for everyone or perhaps a small range of differentials between the highest paid and the lowest, say three to one, and some want to go further and pay extra to those with dependants rather than to those with jobs which are usually higher paid. Others would insist on rates at least as good as those negotiated by trade unions in other parts of the industry. Some academics assume that market forces will assert themselves in one form or another so that people will only join co-operatives if the rate of pay and hopes of profits, balanced by other factors, such as a congenial atmosphere and more control over one's job,

10. See page 83 et seq.
11. See page 26.

are more attractive than available alternatives. Then there is the question whether members should have to make a capital contribution on joining. Some argue that such a contribution is necessary to engender a real commitment to the enterprise, while others think it wrong that members should have to risk their savings as well as their jobs in the one enterprise. However, the probability is that without some contribution from everyone, equal or according to salary, the business will not be economically viable. Linked to the question of capital contribution is the right of members to draw out their capital, and a share of capital appreciation, on their retirement. Some are firmly against payment out of capital appreciation to individual members, whether obtained by building up general reserves out of profits or by appreciation in value of particular assets. Those with this attitude may well choose an ICOM constitution, but, even so, there is nothing to stop ICOM firms from making golden handshakes to retiring members and they will in any case repay capital contributions made by members by way of loans. If they prefer to use one of our constitutions, there is nothing to prevent them from building up general reserves, refraining from paying out sums in respect of capital appreciation and, on winding up, passing the necessary resolution to give surplus assets to any organisation authorised by the constitution. Some would put the emphasis on making socially useful products, producing to meet needs rather than working for profit. However, this may well depend on the availability of capital from a source willing to accept less than the market rate. It is often said that co-operatives should have social objects as well as working for the benefit of the members. Whatever their attitude or ideology, they should find nothing in our constitution to prevent the business being carried on in any of the ways outlined above[12].

Management and Accountability

There is nothing in our constitutions to dictate how the business shall be managed apart from following the statutory requirements that there shall be a committee in the case of societies and a board of directors in the case of companies. Neither do conventional companies normally make any further provision and they have developed a very wide range of management styles from very autocratic to very participative. In the case of conventional companies the directors are accountable to the shareholders who have appointed them and who can dismiss them at any time. In the case of worker-controlled firms

12. See Chapter 2.

the committee or the directors are accountable to the whole worker membership who have equally appointed them and can dismiss them. The major problem that arises is how to make this accountability a reality. In small co-operatives the management functions are often rotated amongst members and all decisions of any importance are made at general meetings. However, in most firms this is not possible owing to the specialist skills required in different parts of the operation and the specialist skills of management whether in production, finance or marketing. It appears that the eventual dominance of these specialist and managerial grades is a common experience of worker-controlled businesses.

The members want these skills to be exercised so that the firm stays in business, pays proper wages and builds up enough reserves to weather bad years. But the members will also want the personal side of management to be carried out effectively so that due weight is given to members' desires for job autonomy, training, career prospects, a good work environment, pleasant human relationships and health and safety. The balance between earning more and enjoying a rewarding occupation should be for the members, not management, to decide. A well known experiment in accountability was carried out in the post war years by the Glacier Metal Co. Ltd. Over many years of trial and error detailed rules were drawn up covering a representative system based on works committees and councils through which management was made responsible to the wishes of the work force[13]. These rules were entirely outside the Memorandum and Articles of Association and in the same way any worker-controlled firm can make its own detailed rules covering the accountability of management to the whole membership. Very important features must be the method of fixing the salaries of managers, of selecting them and of dismissing them. The power that the membership in general have over the careers and prospects of managers must be a powerful inducement to managers to carry out the wishes of the membership or to explain fully why it is impossible to do so. It is sometimes objected that on conversion of a business from a conventional company to a worker-controlled one the same managers continue with their same bad habits. However, with the change of constitution, the managers' obligation to satisfy the shareholders is changed to an obligation to satisfy the whole membership, which must make a difference to the managers' attitudes. And not all managers have bad habits. The Glacier Metal Company was not alone in trying to

---

13. See *Exploration in Management* by Wilfred Brown, Pelican Books 1965.

develop a better relationship between management and work force with more democracy and participation so that policy is arrived at by discussion and consent rather than imposed by management. This has now become one of the objectives of progressive management training[14].

Trade Union Roles

At the CRU Conference Alan Oberman of the Royal Arsenal Co-operative Society put forward the view that making management accountable was the prime role for trade unions. He pointed out that non-management employees in a firm have great difficulty in researching alternative policies to those favoured by management and that the pressures on management are to give priority to the financial viability and success of the enterprise. He sees a vital necessity for trade unions, first, to take on board the management policies, assess them and weigh them up against different priorities; and also to ensure that workers' wishes and conditions of work are not overlooked in the stress for viability. Another reason for trade union involvement was mentioned arising out of a strike which took place in one of the Mondragon Co-operatives. It arose because one group of workers felt that they were being unfairly treated but they were over-ruled and so went on strike. It may seem likely that in any organisation, other than a very small one, there will be disagreements from time to time between different groups about such matters as work loads, working conditions and pay differentials, all matters which trade unions are in the habit of dealing with. But, nevertheless, some co-operators are confident that the change to worker control puts managers and managed on the same side, and enables a spirit of co-operation to arise which will overcome these problems and make the traditional trade union role unnecessary.

Another role suggested for trade unions was setting up resource centres to promote producer co-operatives, in line with what is already being done by the Wales TUC. The Wales TUC sent a team to Mondragon to see what lessons could be learnt and before publishing its report in 1981; *Co-operation and Job Creation in Wales : A Feasibility Study*. The Resource Centre set up by the Wales TUC is fulfilling part of the function of the Peoples' Bank in Mondragon, which was created by a group of co-operatives and provides both capital and a wide range of business consultancy to the co-operatives associated with it. Any promoting body, trade

14. For information about courses designed specifically for co-operatives, enquiries should be made to the CDA (see note 7 above) and ICOM of Vassalli House, 20 Central Road, Leeds LS1 6DE.

union or otherwise, may well produce their own model constitution but they may find a general purpose model sufficient. At Mondragon the control by the Bank over the way the individual co-operatives conduct their affairs is by a contract entered into before the Bank will give assistance, known as the Contract of Association. No doubt any sponsoring body would insist that the constitution covers the basic requirement of a democratic worker-controlled organisation, but beyond that, the most convenient way of dealing with most questions of policy and practice is probably by a separate contract which can be modified by agreement when circumstances change.

Slow Growth of Producer Co-operatives

Over recent years, there has been renewed academic interest in worker-controlled enterprises and it seems to be generally conceded that there are considerable advantages. But the advantages claimed are predominantly for the workers, not for the entrepreneurs or other owners. They tend to be more satisfying organisations to work in, to create better human relationships and to call forth more loyalty and commitment. But, on the other hand, they often suffer from under-capitalisation and unprofessional management. The academics tend to ask why, if they are potentially superior forms of work organisation, have they not competed successfully in the market place and taken over a larger share of industrial production. If their analysis is correct, the answer must be that the persons who it is claimed will benefit, i.e. the majority of employees, do not know of this possibility or do not believe it will work. Their beliefs are likely to be affected predominantly by the views of their own organisations, the trades unions, which have been ambivalent in their attitude. Support for producer co-operatives is written into the rule books of some trade unions; a number of union branches have promoted, or helped to promote, co-operatives; and now the Wales TUC has set up a Resource Centre. But, on the whole, the trade union movement has been lukewarm to the development of worker-controlled firms in a capitalist society, seeing it as a diversion from their main effort to improve the lot of the majority of their members and seeing it as sometimes leading to self-exploitation and under-cutting agreed union rates.

One academic, Hank Levin[15], suggests that worker-controlled enterprises are discriminated against in capitalist societies; that the legal constitutions and legal provisions in general have been

---

15. In Chapter 3 of *Participatory and Self-Managed Firms, Evaluating Economic Performance* edited by Derek C. Jones and Jan Svejnar, Lexington Books 1982.

formulated to meet the needs of the entrepreneurs and owners of capital; that financial institutions have preferred to finance conventional companies and have been suspicious of worker-controlled firms with which they are unfamiliar; and that we have all been educated to fit in to a hierarchical society, not a participative one. Although raising finance for a venture is always difficult it seems that, whatever about the past, a number of banks and other financial institutions are now giving fair treatment to co-operative ventures. There seems no reason why the Industrial and Commercial Finance Corporation, which has pioneered management buy-outs, should not equally assist worker buy-out[16].

Authoritarian attitudes and behaviour are becoming less dominant in our society and no doubt an increase in worker-controlled enterprises would increase experiment in, and understanding of, participative decision-making. On the legal side, we hope that this book will take its place with other developments in showing how existing legal provisions can be adapted for use by worker-controlled businesses.

Worker Buy-outs as possible Growth Area

If employees in industry and their trade unions do decide that running a co-operative firm is a worthwhile alternative to conventional employment, then it is likely that worker buy-outs will tend to replace management buy-outs. It often suits the parent company to dispose of part of its undertaking; perhaps it took over a firm with several branches but only wants to keep one, or on a re-organisation finds that some parts of its empire no longer fit in. A sale to management or workers is often the company's preferred option and to secure it favourable terms are offered. This gives a very much better start to the new worker-controlled firm than a rescue operation when a conventional company is closing down because it cannot pay its way. In drafting our Memorandum and Articles of Association, we had this situation very much in mind and have allowed for the possibility of a financial institution supporting the buy-out, putting money in on loan or taking up preference shares or even taking a share of profits, but without control[17]. In each case the workers will negotiate the best terms they can but they may prefer to take any of these options rather than fail to raise the purchase price.

16. See page 44.
17. See page 44 et seq.

Chapter 1

Some Existing Constitutions

TRADITIONAL PRODUCER CO-OPERATIVES

Industrial and Provident Societies Acts

Capitalist businesses in the private sector are normally carried on by sole proprietors, by partners or by companies registered under the Companies Acts. Traditional producer co-operatives were registered under the Industrial and Provident Societies Acts which were framed specifically to provide an alternative form of incorporation for co-operative societies to that provided for companies. Shareholding in co-operative societies registered under these Acts has always been subject to a limit which is currently £10,000.[1]

The first Industrial and Provident Societies Act was in 1852 which provided registration with the Registrar of Friendly Societies (Friendly Societies were provident societies already subject to registration). Registration under this Act gave incorporation as a legal form but left the members with unlimited personal liability for the debts of the Society. The Act of 1862 conferred limited liability in the same way as limited liability had then recently been permitted for companies under the Limited Liability Act, 1855. In each case the liability of members was limited to the amount of their shareholding (or their guarantee in the case of a company limited by guarantee) so that, once this contribution was made, a member could not be forced to make any further payment to the company or society even if it was insolvent.

The Industrial and Provident Societies Acts permit registration by a society for carrying on any industry, business or trade whether wholesale or retail in two circumstances only. The first is if it is a bona fide co-operative society. The second circumstance is if the business of the society is being conducted for the benefit of

1. Industrial and Provident Societies (Increase in Shareholding Limit) Order 1981, S1 1981 No.395.

the community and there are special reasons why the society should be registered as a society rather than as a company under the Companies Acts. A society registered under the Industrial and Provident Societies Acts may not call itself a company. This follows from the provision in S.53(5) of the I & PS Act 1965 that on conversion of a company to a society the name shall not include the word 'company' but there is no similar statutory prohibition of a company being registered with a name which includes the word 'co-operative'. However, at the time of writing the Registrar of Companies and the Registrar of Friendly Societies are considering the circumstances in which the word 'co-operative' might be accepted as part of the name of a registered company.

The Acts do not say what is a bona fide co-operative society but the Registrar of Friendly Societies does provide his guidelines as follows:

"There is no statutory definition of a bona fide co-operative society but such a society will normally be expected to satisfy the following conditions:-

(a) *Conduct of business.*
The business of the society will be conducted for the mutual benefit of its members in such a way that the benefit which members obtain will in the main stem from their participation in its business. Such participation may vary in accordance with the nature of the society. It may consist of purchasing from or selling to the society, of using the services or amenities provided by it or of supplying services to carry out its business.

(b) *Control.*
Control of the society will under its rules be vested in the members equally and not in accordance with their financial interest in the society. In general therefore, the principle of 'one man one vote' must obtain.

(c) *Interest on share and loan capital.*
Interest payable on share and loan capital will under its rules not exceed a rate necessary to obtain and retain the capital required to carry out the objects of the society. The appropriate rate may vary from time to time between societies of different classes and according to the term and security of loans.

Section 1(3) of the Act provides that a society which carries on business with the object of making profits mainly for the payment of interest, dividends or bonuses on money invested with or lent to the society or any other person is not a bona fide co-operative society.

(d) *Profits.*
The profits of the society's business after payment of interest on share capital, if distributable amongst the members, will under its rules be distributable amongst them in relation to the extent to which they have traded with or taken part in the business of the society. Thus in a retail trading society or an agricultural marketing society profits will be distributable amongst members as a dividend or bonus on purchases from or sales to the society. In some societies (as for example social clubs) profits will not usually be distributable amongst members but are ploughed back to cheapen and improve the amenities available to members.

(e) *Restriction on membership.*
There should be no artificial restriction of membership with the object of increasing the value of proprietary rights and interest. There may, of course, be grounds for restricting membership that do not offend the co-operative principle; for example, the membership of a club might be limited by the size of its premises and of a self-build housing society by the number of houses that could be erected on a particular site."

There is no direct reference in these guidelines to producer co-operatives although there is to a retail trading society, an agricultural marketing society, to social clubs and self-build housing societies. Of course, producer co-operatives do fit in as employees supply services to the society to help it carry out its business but one has to wonder whether producer co-operatives were particularly in mind when co-operatives were first given their own distinctive legal shape.

In 1852, when the first Industrial and Provident Societies Act was passed, co-operative societies were already in existence and had been for some time. Not being able to incorporate themselves as a legal person they presumably carried on business as unincorporated societies with unlimited liability of the officers, the committee or the members according to circumstances. Probably the best known of them were the Rochdale Pioneers, formed in 1844, whose co-operative store was in Toad Lane, Rochdale. They formulated rules which became a model for other societies and must have been very much in the minds of the framers of the Act in 1852. The rules included one member one vote irrespective of shareholding, open membership, a fixed or limited rate of interest on capital and surplus profit to be distributed to members as a dividend in proportion to their purchases.

Producer Co-operatives

It was not until 1854, two years after the first Act had been passed, that the Pioneers formed a producer co-operative, 'The Co-operative Manufacturing Society', which was successful and expanded. In doing so it raised capital from people who were not working for the society and they became a large majority of members and by 1862 had converted the society into a conventional company.[2] Conversions between societies and companies can be done by a comparatively simple procedure if 75% of the members pass the necessary resolution. This was an early example of what is often referred to in the co-operative movement as a co-operative enterprise degenerating into a capitalist one and it adds to the impression that the framework for co-operation set up by the Acts are better suited to consumer and marketing co-operatives than to producer co-operatives. As we know, the main thrust of the co-operative movement went into consumer co-operatives, though some marketing co-operatives, such as in agriculture, and Housing Societies have also flourished. In fact the producer co-operatives felt so neglected by the Co-operative Union that in 1882 they formed their own organisation, the Co-operative Productive Federation (CPF). The producer movement continued to grow, reaching their greatest numbers in the 1890s. According to tables prepared by Derek C. Jones[3] there were over 100 in existence by the early '90s which number never exceeded 120 and dropped by 1908 to 92 and in 1924 to 69. It is believed that by 1973 there were only 16 surviving with very few new formations. In 1980, the administration of the CPF was taken over by the Co-operative Union.

The Acts provided a legal framework for a group of people to carry out an enterprise which they all wanted to be carried out. The sort of situation that arises spontaneously when people form social and sports clubs and all manner of special interest societies. Consumer co-operatives had also arisen spontaneously in an effort to cut the cost of shopping by taking over the role of the retailer and, with it, his profit. The individual investment is not

---

2. *Workers Co-operatives, Jobs and Dreams* by Jenny Thornley, Heinemann Educational Books, 1981.
3. *The New Worker Co-operatives* edited Ken Coates, Spokesman, 1976.

very great and, indeed, has always been limited by law and in most cases the investor is happy to receive a limited return on the investment because of the value received in cheaper goods or other benefits of belonging to the co-operative. The people to benefit are the members who join by buying shares. Normal business relationships can be entered into with everyone else, premises bought or rented, money borrowed from banks and employees hired and fired. In fact, within the co-operative movement, here and in many countries, there is a strong commitment to social goals, but they are not a necessary part of the legal framework provided by the Acts. One may conjecture that the framework meets the needs of the members very satisfactorily when the providers of capital and the users of the services are predominantly the same people and when there is no great temptation to wind up the enterprise and take a large capital gain.

In the case of producer co-operatives these two conditions tend to diminish with time. Members retire or leave and the society cannot afford to repay their shareholding or the shareholding of their family or friends, so the number of non-employee members increases. According to a table compiled by Jones, only 16% of producer societies making returns to the Co-operative Union in 1936 had more than 50% employee members and by 1970 this had dropped to 4%. During the same period the proportion of employees who were members was 75% in 1936, dropping to 54% in 1970. So, in 1936, 75% membership of employees gave control in only 16% of societies.

For employee members their society is not concerned with some peripheral activity but with their livelihood, representing their main business activity. Those who have worked hard and co-operatively to build up a flourishing business may very properly want some benefit when they retire. Merely to keep their shareholding at its nominal value and with a fixed limited return may seem very inadequate when profits have been ploughed back for years instead of being distributed, thereby creating a capital value very much in excess of nominal shareholding. In the case of employee members who retire, it is quite possible to recognise their services with a golden handshake or pension or both, which could be perfectly satisfactory but is not always done. But in the case of non-employee members who see the capital value exceed the nominal shareholding many times over, either by profits ploughed back or appreciation of capital assets, there must be a temptation to wind up and share in the increased value rather than continue to receive a small fixed dividend.

Conflicting Interests of Employee and Non-Employee Members

This conflict of interest between employee, or participating, member and non-participating member is built in to the constitution as laid down by the Acts. In the ordinary business enterprise, capital, i.e. the owner or owners, or company controlled by the owners, hires labour and, having paid labour the agreed wages, keeps any profit. When the expression 'producer co-operative' or even more so 'worker co-operative' is heard, it might easily be assumed that this situation was reversed so that labour hires capital and keeps in its own hands both the control of the enterprise and the allocation of profits. But this is not what the Acts have done. They have left control with capital in the sense that members exercise control, and membership comes about by subscribing for shares, however small a holding may be permitted, although the manner in which they exercise control is circumscribed.

In general, each member is to have one vote regardless of shareholding, the benefits given to members are to stem, in the main, from their participation in the business, profits are to be distributed on the same principle and interest on shares is not to exceed a rate necessary to obtain and retain the capital required. So those members who are not participating have to join in a policy of running the business for the benefit of the participators. Part of that policy may well be to build up the business by ploughing back profits so that the firm keeps up with modern methods and equipment, keeps, or expands, its markets and pays good wages and bonuses to the participating members. This increase in value is of no benefit to the non-employee member unless the society is wound up and the surplus assets are distributed amongst the shareholders in proportion to their shareholding. Although it is considered to be against co-operative principles to divide surplus assets according to shareholding nevertheless it can be done if there is a 75% majority in favour.

Of course, there is always a temptation to sell any business if the rate of profits shows a sufficiently poor return on the value of the assets, but in the case of a producer co-operative this situation is artificially exaggerated by the co-operative framework. It would be reduced considerably for the non-employee members if either their rate of interest went up with the increasing value of the enterprise or if they were entitled only to their nominal capital back on a dissolution. In the first case their rewards would more nearly correspond to those of an ordinary shareholder in a conventional company and in the latter to a preference shareholder. In either case, a winding up would release their capital but it would not make a dramatic difference to the return they could get on re-investment.

NEW WAVE CO-OPERATIVES OR COMMON OWNERSHIPS

Worker Controlled Businesses with Labour hiring Capital

For whatever reason, the old-style producer co-operative movement which started in the last century was very much in decline by the 1960s. But the new wave producer co-operatives were already being pioneered by the Industrial Common Ownership Movement (ICOM)[4] which was formed in 1958 as the Society for Democratic Integration in Industry (Demintry) and changed its name in 1971. Although providing model rules for registration under the Industrial and Provident Societies Acts, ICOM have modified the framework to secure that, in effect, labour hires capital. Apart from founder members only employees may become members and their membership ceases with their employment. At about the same time in the mid '50s, the Mondragon Co-operatives were starting in Spain and they also developed a model constitution under which labour was to hire capital. Membership is restricted to employees and, in practice, nearly all employees become members in spite of a normal requirement for a substantial capital contribution.

It seems that modern co-operators here and in Mondragon want a constitution which provides for labour hiring capital and so the framework provided by the Industrial and Provident Societies Acts has to be modified by the rules of the Society. Once this situation is reached there is no need to restrict registration to the Industrial and Provident Societies Acts, if the standard memorandum and articles of association for registration as a company under the Companies Acts can equally well be modified. ICOM have already come to this conclusion and in 1981 they produced a model Memorandum and Articles for registration as a company limited by guarantee without any share capital. There is no reason why a company limited by shares should not also be suitably modified.

But once registration as a company is recognised as an acceptable alternative it can be misleading to talk of producer co-operatives and better to refer to worker-controlled enterprises or businesses. The requirements for such an enterprise as they are now evolving, will include many aspects of the Registrar's guide

---

4. Industrial Common Ownership Movement (ICOM) Ltd. Vassalli House, 20 Central Road, Leeds LS1 6DE.

to a bona fide co-operative but with important modifications. They appear to be on the following lines:

1. A controlling interest shall be vested in employee members for the time being so that non-employee members, if any, shall never get control.
2. Voting by employee members shall be on the basis of one person one vote.
3. Interest or other rewards to capital will not exceed a rate found necessary to obtain and retain the capital required by the enterprise.
4. Profits, after meeting the entitlement of non-employee members, if any, shall be distributed or put to reserves as determined by the members.
5. Membership shall be open to all adult employees subject only to any reasonable exceptions which may be required covering, for example, a short probationary period or temporary or part-time employees.

These requirements call for a modification of the statutory framework of a society or a company to ensure that employee members have control and that on ceasing to be employed they lose their vote. In the case of a company it calls also for a modification of the conventional constitution to ensure that there are always shares available for issue to new employees and that voting by employee members shall be on the basis of one person one vote. But in addition, there is the practical problem which is well recognised in the producer co-operative movement here and elsewhere which concerns the destination of ploughed back profits and capital appreciation in general.

Business success will almost certainly demand substantial ploughing back of profits for modernisation and expansion. Co-operators who plough back rather than take out all they can are likely to want some stake in the ploughed back profits with the right to withdraw their share on retirement. If withdrawals on retirement are too great the enterprise may not be able to find the money without selling assets and running down or closing the business. If withdrawals are too little, this may discourage necessary ploughing back or lead to a very large increase in capital value and a consequent temptation to the co-operators to sell the enterprise and realise the gain.

ICOM Models
ICOM have taken the bull by the horns and virtually dispensed with share capital. Apart from founder members, membership is

confined to employees who cease to be members on termination of their employment. One £1 share is both the maximum and minimum shareholding which is cancelled on termination of membership. The shares carry no right to dividend or bonus, so that a share becomes little more than a ticket of membership. Any capital put in by members, or by anyone else, is put in as loan capital with or without an issue of loan stock. Each society is free to agree terms for loans including the date of repayment, if any, as loan stock need not be redeemable. The rate of interest is subject to maximum rates specified in the model rules. As nearly all new wave co-operatives are formed under ICOM rules, they must work in practice, although it might be feared that the absence of share capital would inhibit borrowing. The new co-operatives are predominantly very small so it may well be that banks and other lenders require guarantees from the co-operators in the same way as they often do from directors of family companies. Once reserves are built up from retained profits, they will form a core of risk capital which should make borrowing easier.

ICOM model rules deal with the destination of reserves by providing that on a winding up any surplus assets shall not be distributed among the members but shall go to another common ownership enterprise or central fund or to charity. It is this rule and the rule limiting membership to employees which constitutes the distinctive features of a common ownership enterprise as opposed to any other type of co-operative enterprise. It is an expression of the view that a successful co-operative should be handed on from generation to generation, rather than built up only to be sold to the capitalist sector for the personal gain of the members[5]. The rule applies only to reserves and not to profits retained on members' loan accounts by notionally distributing to members and then borrowing back from them. Such loan accounts can be repayable on retirement so encouraging members to agree to adequate ploughing back. There is no reason either why the enterprise should not provide pensions and adopt a policy of golden handshakes on retirement. The allocation of ploughed back profits between general reserves and members' loan accounts and the payment of pension and capital sums on retirement are for the members to decide. They will have to strike a balance between the conflicting needs of the older retiring members who will want money out and the younger ones who do not want to see the economic viability of

---

5. It is understood from ICOM that the rule gives comfort to public authorities making grants to Co-operatives who can reinforce the rule by specifying repayment or conversion to loan should the rule be changed.

the enterprise undermined by depletion of capital.

This system of protecting general reserves from distribution to members on a winding up is not as binding as it looks. It is common to find such a clause in the constitution of a charitable or non-profit making organisation and in those cases the clause is legally enforceable. Money will have been obtained for the purposes of the organisation, not for the benefit of the members, so that any distribution amongst themselves would be a misappropriation of funds which could lead to criminal or civil proceedings. But in the case of a common ownership enterprise the money put to reserves is money which the members could have distributed amongst themselves if they wished, so they are quite free to get round the rule if they so desire.

It is quite accepted by ICOM that the rule is an expression of intention which can be changed later if a sufficient majority of members wish to change it. A 75% majority can change the rule itself. A simple majority could decide to sell the assets and distribute all profits from the sale and profits brought forward as reserves, before agreeing to support a resolution to wind up which needs a 75% majority.

A convenient legal method of safeguarding reserves would be to allocate them as shares to trustees to hold on whatever trusts were desired. But the choice by ICOM of the Industrial and Provident Societies Act framework or a company limited by guarantee make this difficult. A company limited by guarantee may no longer have any share capital and the value of shares held in societies is limited, currently at £10,000. The Trustees would count as one shareholder and so be subject to the limit unless the Trustees were a society or societies themselves registered under the Industrial and Provident Societies Acts. However, it is hard to see how acting as trustee of a society's reserves could be accepted as a business registerable as a co-operative society. But if the enterprise was registered as a company limited by shares, there would be no problem in issuing non-voting shares to trustees so capitalising some of the reserves and making their distribution impossible otherwise than under the terms of the Trust.

Mondragon Co-operatives and Job Ownership Ltd. (JOL)

A large majority of the Mondragon Co-operatives have developed their response to the problems of control and destination of reserves collectively. They got together and set up their own banking and general support organisation, the Caja Laboral Popular (CLP), or People's Savings Bank, which began to operate in 1960. The Bank has flourished and is now a large organisation providing not only capital but a wide range of consultancy on market research, product development, management and financial control[6]. But in order to benefit from the Bank's loans or advice the co-operative has to enter into a contract with it, the Contract of Association. Under this contract the co-operative surrenders a substantial part of its autonomy but, at the same time, acquires the right to representation in the General Assembly of the Bank which is a secondary co-operative formed by the co-operatives to help them consolidate and expand. The associating co-operative agrees to carry out all banking and financial operations through the Bank and to make available to the Bank so much of its own capital as may be determined by the Bank's General Assembly. It also undertakes to comply with a set of basic principles regarding employment creation, capital ownership, earnings differentials, distribution of surplus and democratic organisation. Only employees may be members and apart from special cases, such as temporary employees, all employees are encouraged to join. Of the capital contribution made on joining part is put to general reserves and is non-returnable. This part may not exceed 25% and is typically 15%. Profits are allocated between general reserves, a social fund and members' capital accounts. The members' capital accounts are repayable within four years of retirement. General reserves will not be distributed to members unless, presumably, there is a change of policy by the Bank.

The success of the Mondragon co-operatives stimulated the setting up in this country in 1978 of Job Ownership Ltd. (JOL)[7], a non-profit making company limited by guarantee. JOL was formed to encourage and assist the ownership and control of industrial and service enterprises by the people who work in them rather than by the people who supply them with money. They have looked for ways of incorporating some of the salient features of the Mondragon Contract of Association into the constitution of the enterprise but have come up against a basic legal difficulty. That is that the constitution sets out the objects of the enterprise, its capital, its membership and its power structure, but cannot determine how that power is to be exercised. The law of the land contains many detailed provisions about what a company or society may or may not do, as well as the general law affecting us all, and lays down penalties or other methods of enforcement. Also a company can enter into an enforceable contract to do or refrain from doing this, that or the

6. *Mondragon: An Economic Analysis* by Henk Thomas and Chris Logan, George Allen and Unwin, 1982.
7. Job Ownership Ltd. of 9 Poland Street, London, W1V 3DG.

other in return for some benefits, in which case the other contracting party can enforce the contract, as does the People's Bank in Mondragon. But, in general, a company may manage its affairs as it thinks fit and can change any restrictions in its articles of association by a 75% majority. So there is not much point in putting in elaborate provisions concerning differentials in pay, allocations to reserves or non-distribution on winding up unless the co-operators themselves positively want them.

Today's co-operators will probably want a legal form which safeguards the five principles set out above, leaving the co-operators the maximum flexibility in how they run the enterprise. They can then seek what guidance and help they want on such matters as pay differentials, management structure, democratic control, destination of reserves and financial management which they can experiment with and change from time to time as seems expedient.

CONVENTIONAL BUSINESSES

Partnerships

It may assist to look at the constitutional forms of conventional business enterprises with which the co-operators will find themselves competing. Apart from the sole proprietor, the oldest form is a partnership in which two or more people go into business either for a particular project or on a continuing basis. Except in the rare cases of limited partnerships, all the partners are liable without limit for partnership debts and partners are held out as having authority to bind the partnership in matters within their normal business practice. This unlimited liability and implied authority to partners to make contracts binding the other partners makes it most unlikely that open membership to all employees would ever be a reality. In practice, a fairly high degree of common interest and outlook is necessary for the smooth functioning of a partnership and it is normal for the partnership to employ others. On the whole, partnerships are comparatively small when compared to businesses in general and their number is limited by the Companies Acts to 20, with exceptions covering a wide range of professional partnerships where there is no limit on numbers. A partnership is not a legal person but a collection of individuals bound together by contract and subject to the Partnership Acts. Partners may have an equal or unequal share in the business and the profits and losses and may have one vote per partner or some system of weighting. Interest may be paid on capital contributed by the partners or not, as they wish. All the rights of the partners between themselves may be regulated by their partnership agreement though the Acts lay down the terms that will be assumed in the absence of any agreement to the contrary.

When a new partner joins a new partnership agreement is entered into, although the document may be a short one referring to the existing agreement. On retirement, partners will expect to take out their share of capital although it is common to allow the continuing partners to pay by instalments over a few years. It is usual to allow the retiring partner or the continuing partners to call for a revaluation of major assets, usually the partnership premises, before calculating the share of the outgoing partner. The need to pay out retiring partners requires continual foresight in managing the partnership affairs. Reserves need to be built up or sufficient borrowing capacity left unused or some insurance taken out. It is not uncommon for partners to agree to take out a pension policy which allows them to borrow their anticipated contribution to the next retirement. Of course a new partner replacing the retiring one might bring in sufficient capital to pay him out but this is unlikely. New partners will probably make a contribution, which is often borrowed for the purpose, but will then leave some profits undrawn for some years until their capital account is equivalent to that of the other partners. At the same time the oldest partners may be paid out more each year, so reducing the burden on their retirement. The problem of paying out retiring partners and getting capital from new ones has been sufficiently difficult for members of some professions, e.g. solicitors, largely giving up payments for goodwill. It used to be normal to pay for goodwill on joining a partnership and be paid back when retiring, the amount being about one and a half to two years' share of profits, although the amount varied considerably. As so few new entrants can afford such a payment on top of their contribution to capital it is now widely felt that retiring partners do not need a payment for goodwill if they have contributed adequately to a pension fund. Contributions qualify for tax exemption up to a substantial limit and some partnership agreements contain a clause requiring partners to contribute, so that when the time comes they are more likely to retire without undue stress.

Company limited by Shares

The legal structure in most general use in business today is the company limited by shares and registered under the Companies Acts. The company is a separate legal person which binds itself on formal occasions by its seal. At other times a director, the secretary or another employee may be authorised to sign on behalf of the company. But, naturally, there is no implied authority for members to enter into contracts for the company, as partners can for their partnership. In fact, the members' role may be quite passive as the management of the company is in the hands of the board of directors. The company seal is used on the authority of the board and third parties can safely deal with the directors knowing that they have the power to bind the company in running the business authorised by the company's objects clause.

The members elect the directors and can remove them at any time, so, although the members cannot interfere in the day to day running of the business, they can tell the directors what they want done and dismiss them if they fail to carry it out. Membership is by shareholding, so in order to become a member a person must buy shares from an existing shareholder or have shares allotted to him by the company. There is no question of open membership as membership is strictly limited to those people who are the present owners of the shares which have been issued. A person becomes a new member simply by acquiring shares as the membership rights then follow from the memorandum and articles of association. There is no new agreement between all existing members and the new member as in a partnership although the articles of association are in the nature of an agreement between the company and each member. The member's liability is limited to the nominal value of the share, so once this has been fully paid after its original allotment, there is nothing further to pay even if the company becomes insolvent and is wound up.

On first registration, the company will state in its Memorandum and Articles of Association the amount of its authorised capital on which capital duty will be paid. Shares may then be issued for value up to the amount authorised but there is no need to issue to the full authorised amount. The authorised capital may be increased at any time on registering the increase and paying the extra duty. The constitution may authorise the issue of a wide variety of shares which are broadly divided into ordinary shares and preference shares. The preference shareholders will typically receive a fixed rate of interest and be entitled to repayment of the nominal value on winding up in preference to the ordinary shareholders but will not normally have any voting rights. The ordinary shareholders typically control the company, voting according to the value of their shareholding and being entitled to all profits after paying the preference shareholders their due. A company may issue a number of different classes of preference and ordinary shares with different rights, including ordinary shares without voting rights.

If ordinary shareholders agree to plough back profits, it will increase the chance of bigger dividends from bigger profits in the future and on a winding up will increase the value of residual assets to be distributed amongst them. This expectation of higher dividends resulting from ploughing back profits increases the market value of ordinary shares in a prosperous company, unlike the shares in a co-operative society which have a fixed rate of interest however great the residual value of the shares becomes. It follows that an ordinary shareholder is less tempted to wind up the company in order to realise a capital gain as it should be possible to sell the shares to another investor at a comparable figure. In fact, this option to wind up only applies if the shareholder, or group of shareholders, wanting to sell have 75% of voting shares as it requires a special resolution with a 75% majority to force a winding up. A 75% majority wishing to sell their shares can demand the full market value of the goodwill and assets since they have the alternative of winding up and putting the goodwill and assets on the market. But shareholders with a controlling interest, i.e. 51% of the voting shares, can expect a price reflecting the value of the business as a going concern as this is what the purchaser will get control of. A minority shareholder will probably not do so well and will expect to settle for a price based on future dividend expectations. Purchasers who get control are buying more than an investment, they can also get jobs as directors and have the opportunity to run the business their way.

Although a co-operative society may repay shares to members in ordinary circumstances, a company may not. In exchange for the limitation of members' liability to the amount they have put in as share capital there are rigorous provisions to prevent that share capital being paid back to members rather than remaining available for the company's creditors. Ploughed back profits are in a different situation as they will normally be credited to a reserve account and remain available for distribution as dividends unless capitalised as bonus shares. Once capitalised they also cannot easily be distributed. There are provisions for reduction of capital and repayment to members in exceptional circumstances but they involve an application to the High Court and so are hardly for everyday use and sometimes a reduction can be effected by the company buying its own shares (see pp.56 and 57).

No doubt there are some director owners who do all they can to milk the company, but companies would not have reached their present dominant position without owners who are prepared to leave substantial profits in the company thereby settling for capital growth rather than immediate high dividends. How to realise the capital growth, perhaps on death or retirement, depends on the company. If it is a large company with a stock exchange quotation, then the sale of shares is easy. If it is not quoted but is large enough to go on the unlisted securities market, and has chosen to do so, then that market may well find a purchaser. Otherwise a minority shareholder in a private company will probably hope to sell to the directors or existing shareholders. A majority shareholder will put the business on the market, but may have to persuade the remaining shareholders to sell as well as the purchaser may well want all the shares and total control.

Chapter 2

New Model Constitutions

MEMBERS' CAPITAL

Partnership as a Model

The model constitutions set out on p.81 and following incorporate the principles set out on p.26 and also allow the members wide flexibility in their requirements for capital contributions from members and in members' rights to share in the firm's accumulated reserves. At one extreme members may wish to be placed very much in the same position as partners and, at the other, they may be mainly concerned to build up a business with adequate reserves for the benefit of future members and the community as well as of themselves. If the members want to behave like partners they are perfectly free to do so. The problems mentioned on pages 30 and 31, of unlimited liability of all partners, each partner able to bind the firm and cumbersome method of taking in new partners, all disappear on incorporation as a society or a company. Liability becomes limited, only the committee or board of directors, or someone authorised by them, can bind the firm and new members are automatically bound by the constitution.

In the accounts of a partnership each partner has an account which is credited with his or her initial contribution and each year with a share of profits and is debited with amounts drawn out. Sometimes for convenience this account is divided into separate capital and drawings accounts. As a partnership is not a legal entity there is no general reserve account, but all profits are immediately divided amongst the partners and credited to their accounts which, collectively, form part of the firm's reserves. As each partner's liability is unlimited their private assets also form part of the reserves available to pay creditors in case of need. But in the case of a society or limited company any profits paid out to members, even if lent back, no longer belong to the firm and so are not shown in the accounts as available to meet creditors. If the members have made loans to the firm then the members will claim to join other creditors seeking re-payment from the firm, unless some special arrangement was made postponing their claims to those of other creditors.[1] So this means that in the case of a society or company enough reserves to cover working capital requirements must be kept undistributed. If the members wish to behave like partners this could cause a problem. When partners retire the amount due to them is shown clearly on their accounts. If there is a re-valuation of assets this also is reflected in their accounts as a profit or loss. But when a member retires it will not be known what is that member's share of general reserves unless profits which are ploughed back are also provisionally allocated to the members individually.

Members' Reserve Accounts

What we have done is to provide in the co-operative's constitutions for members' reserve accounts, similar to, but not identical with, the capital accounts in the Mondragon co-operatives. We have provided that the firm may, but need not, put the whole or any part of the undistributed profit to a member's reserve account instead of to general reserves. The member's reserve account comprises separate reserve accounts for each member to which is credited the amount that member has notionally contributed to the member's reserve account which would normally be the amount that member would have received had the profit been distributed.[2] Nevertheless, the credit on a member's reserve account does not belong to that member and is not taxed as part of that member's income, but remains the property of the firm and is subject to corporation tax[3]. If there are

---

1. But even in the absence of any such arrangement a liquidator might well invoke S.74(2)(f) of the Insolvency Act 1986 which provides that in a winding up members' claims as members are deferred to ordinary creditors. The section could well apply if the loan accounts represented profit distributions credited to loan accounts.
2. In the case of companies care should be taken to avoid credits to the member's reserve account being regarded as a premium for the member's share as, in that case, it would have to be credited to a share premium account and would not be available either for payment to the member or transfer to general reserves. This is one reason why members should not be required to contribute to their reserve account from their own resources as a condition of membership. Another reason is that if they made such a contribution they would probably want a firmer right to repayment on retirement than they would be prepared to accept in respect of credits to a part of ploughed back profits. We have introduced the concept of members' reserve accounts as a book-keeping device to show by whose efforts that part of reserves carried to the members' reserve account has been built up, but not as indicating any monetary contribution by that member, although monetary contributions are not prohibited.

losses, or for some other reason the members so decide, they can transfer part or the whole of the members' reserve account to general reserves. This can be seen as an alternative to a reduction in salaries and so fairness can be achieved by keeping each member's reserve account at the same proportion of that member's salary so that a percentage cut in salary or a percentage, or total, withdrawal from reserve accounts has the same effect.

It is unlikely that member's reserve accounts will be kept unless it is intended to pay them out on retirement. If the members have a right to be paid out then the payment will be taxed as part of their emoluments. If they have no right but, nevertheless, are paid out in accordance with a voluntary policy of giving golden handshakes then the whole or part of the payment will qualify for the tax relief on such payments.[4] Clearly it is best for members to receive their reserve accounts as a gratuity and get tax relief if they are prepared to risk not being paid out. We have treated the members' reserve accounts as belonging to the firm without the members having any right to be paid out. But in the case of a society we have included in the Rules the power to make rules requiring the society to pay out the members' reserve accounts on retirement. If such rules are made then the tax relief is lost. Even if made there would still be no guarantee that any sums would actually be credited to the members' reserve accounts, or, if credited, would not be taken back later into general reserves by decision of the society's members. We have given no similar option in the case of a company as it is difficult to accommodate within a company framework.

Share Capital and Loans

Apart from this problem over reserves it is quite straightforward for members of a society to put money in and take it out again on retirement as partners do. In the case of societies the money is put in either as share capital or on loan. Share capital belongs to the society and is available to meet its debts[5], so banks or other creditors may well like to see substantial share capital. As only employees may be individual members it is necessary to terminate their membership immediately on retirement which can only be done by redeeming their shares. As this may cause a cash problem we have given the committee power to convert all or some of the shares to loan account on

---

3. See page 72.
4. See page 72.
5. See page 35 above regarding the standing of members' loans.

retirement and we have given a general meeting power to make rules regarding the repayment of loan accounts. Partnership agreements often provide for the repayment of capital by instalments over a year or two. It may be that a society will prefer to have only nominal shareholdings and rely instead on member's loan accounts. In that case it is possible that a proposed creditor will insist that each member agrees that their loan will not be repaid without the creditor's consent while the creditor's debt is still outstanding.

The situation with a company is different as a company cannot repay shares at will as can a society, although it can now purchase its own shares.[6] We have provided for a special class of shares reserved for employee members only and we have given the company power to fix a minimum holding, which could be a stated amount or by reference to salary or some other criterion. Voting is reserved to the holders of these employee shares who are still employed and is on the basis of one person one vote. On cessation of employment the directors may insist on the transfer of the shares at par to their nominee who might be a new employee or perhaps trustees of an employee trust[7] or even the company.

This makes the employee shares very similar to shares in an I & PS Act society except that voting rights cease with the termination of employment so control cannot pass to non-employee members even if shares are retained when employment ends. The shares would still rank for dividends but we have limited the rate of interest which can be paid on these shares. In a small company members may well prefer to limit shareholding to one share per member so as to avoid the difficulty of disposing of shares after termination of employment. Although the company can insist on a sale to their nominee there is no guarantee that there will be anyone able and willing to buy. In a larger company if employee shares are held in an approved profit sharing scheme the trustees will need to buy more from time to time.[8] Also in a larger company employees might take up preference shares if satisfied that there was a market for them. An employee trust might be a willing purchaser. There is great flexibility in the company structure to enable each enterprise to decide on its own share capital which could include an issue, or issues, of redeemable shares. If the members decide against more than a nominal shareholding then their capital contribution can be by loans and building up reserve accounts, with the loan

6. See page 33.
7. See page 40.
8. See page 74.

accounts postponed, if necessary, to some outside creditors.[9]

Co-operative Model

Members may well feel that a conventional partnership does not provide the right guide-lines for them, but that they want to develop their own specifically co-operative model in which their individual needs are balanced by social concerns, the needs of future members and the spread of worker-control. These views are often expressed in the producer co-operative movement and, indeed, partnerships also often display social concern and pass on the business to the next generation at less than its full market value.[10] We have, accordingly, given wide powers in the constitutions to make gifts for social or charitable purposes as well as to pay, or provide for, pensions for retired members and their dependants. These powers are designed to cover payments for social purposes including the support of other worker-controlled firms or any organisation promoting or assisting them. As mentioned earlier, ICOM have gone further and provided in their constitutions that on a winding up residual assets shall not go to members but to another common ownership enterprise or central fund or to charity. We have provided that they shall go as decided by the members at the time, but in the absence of any resolution shall go to members and recent ex-members in accordance with their reserve accounts and length of service with a note that it may be desired to reflect the level of salary as well.

General Reserves

The question of how much general reserves should be built up for the benefit of future members gives rise to much discussion amongst producer co-operatives. It is clearly a big advantage in running a business to have the use of substantial assets or money without paying any rent or interest on them. There must be many conventional family companies where this is the situation and the principal shareholders know that if they sold out, invested the proceeds and took a job they would be financially much better off. However, they often consider that running the business is a more satisfying way of life provided it brings in a sufficient income. Of course, there are other cases where the money put to reserves is used profitably and results in high dividends on the ordinary shares. If large reserves have been built up but they produce only small profits then sooner or later there is pressure to sell or wind up, either just to realise the gain or in response to a

9. See page 36.
10. See pages 30 and 31.

pressing take-over bid. Many feel that a comfortable position is reached when enough profits are put to reserves each year to create an adequate cushion against bad times, reasonable dividends are paid and there is not too much pressure on prices or wages. In those circumstances minority ordinary shareholders wishing to sell will expect substantially less than the asset value of their holding but probably not so little as to feel too hard done by. A worker-controlled firm also has to find a comfortable balance if it is to avoid eventual pressure to wind up and retiring members feeling that they are not getting a fair share of capital after all they have put in.

Capitalising General Reserves in an Employees' Trust

If members of a worker-controlled company (as opposed to a society) have built up general reserves which they do not want future members to be able to withdraw they can capitalise them by making a bonus issue of shares, which could be employee shares or preference shares, in the names of trustees.[11] At the same time a trust deed would have to be drawn up, and we have provided a model for this. We have made members, ex-members and their immediate families and dependants the beneficiaries during the period of the trust with an option to include charities during this period. We have given the trustees as an optional clause, a discretion to dispose of capital as well as of income which may be felt to be risky but it would be useful if at some time members could not carry on and had to sell or wind up, or some other unforseen circumstances arose.

We have provided for a fixed trust period not exceeding 80 years, which is the longest fixed period permitted by law[12] but with an option to include a provision that the trust terminates twelve months after the company is wound up. On termination of the trusts there are a number of options but the particular ones chosen will have to go into the trust deed at the beginning. The capital could go to such beneficiaries as the trustees decide, or to special classes of beneficiaries, e.g. those then employed by the company, or to the company itself, or to a sponsoring body as part of a bargain with that body, or to charity. If the capital goes to the company itself then insofar as it is still represented by its own preference shares they would then have to be cancelled and the nominal value put to a share redemption reserve account in the books of the company. The company could make a new issue of shares to replace those cancelled and either re-settle them or give

11. See page 28.
12. Sec.1 of the Perpetuities and Accumulations Act, 1964.

them to members as part of profit sharing. If no new issue was made the share redemption reserve would remain as a part of the company's reserves that could not be distributed in cash unless the company was wound up. So, once again, pressure to wind up could arise if the amount of shares transferred to the trustees over the years came to a very large sum[13]. On the other hand, if the size and objects of the trust had proved satisfactory to the members, they would probably re-settle on similar terms, or they might just leave the capital frozen on the share redemption reserve account and make income payments direct to beneficiaries without going through trustees.

We have put forward this trust deed as a method of capitalising reserves on the basis that there can be good commerical reasons for doing so collectively. But the Revenue may challenge the commercial reasons and maintain that the settlement is intended to confer gratuitous benefits on beneficiaries other than the members themselves who direct the company to make the settlement. An advance clearance can be applied for under S.464 of the Taxes Act 1970. The commercial reason could be that a sponsoring body which was conferring real benefits on the company made such a settlement a condition of its help. But, apart from this, it is fairly widely believed that a lack of incentive to build up sufficient reserves to help finance expansion and new technology is a weakness of the co-operative model, as discussed in Chapter 1. ICOM constitutions prohibit, and the Contract of Association of the People's Bank in Mondragaon limit, the right of members to surplus assets on winding up. On the continent there are statutory prohibitions to the distribution of some reserves to members but also statutory benefits given to producer co-operatives. The Mondragon Co-operatives allow members to build up capital accounts which they will receive on retirement, and ICOM constitutions permit members to build up loan accounts by lending back part of their entitlement to profits and they do not prohibit golden handshakes on retirement.

There seem to be two disincentives to ploughing back substantial reserves. One is that the members who allow large profits to go to general reserves obtain no direct claim to any part of those reserves; another is that the next generation of co-operators may decide to distribute them amongst themselves. We have sought to provide a flexible means of response to this dilemma by two innovations: first we have provided for members' reserve accounts, which can be used as a measure for golden handshakes on retirement and so establish a moral claim

---

13. If there were sufficient liquid assets an application could be made to the court for a reduction of capital and payment out to members.

to a defined part of the reserves; secondly we have drafted an employee trust deed, not as a vehicle for the bounty of shareholders to the company's employees, but as a means whereby the members can capitalise some of the profits to which they are entitled on a collective basis. From the point of view of each member this sacrifice may well encourage others to agree and thereby improve the economic performance of the company as a long term employer paying good salaries for the benefit of all members including the settlors. Of course, reserves could be capitalised in the traditional way by being issued to members as bonus shares and this may often be the appropriate means. But with the difficulty of selling shares in a small company the members may well prefer to have an employee trust which could be of real help to them and their dependants in time of need.

If the Revenue insist that the commercial reasons are not sufficient and that the settlement is a transfer of value for inheritance tax purposes, then it is quite possible that the tax can be avoided by bringing it within an available exemption. The exemption for employee trusts is discussed in Chapter 4, which is concerned with the gift of a conventional company to the employees which is not done for commercial reasons. Our model is drafted to come within this exemption, if available, but this could give rise to problems. The exemption to tax on making the settlement is lost if the trust deed permits capital to be applied for the benefit of a five per cent participator at any time during the trust period or afterwards. In the case of a small company some or all of the members will inevitably be five per cent participators unless there are more than 20 members and even then some of them may be. If it is intended to provide for capital going to members who are five per cent participators or back to the company, which would benefit such participators, then the exemption is lost and the clause in the settlement prohibiting such payments would have to be excluded. However, if it is intended that the members, including five percent participators, should receive income only and that the capital goes on termination of the trusts to charity or some other body then the exemption can be claimed.

This exemption, contained in S.13 of the Inheritance Tax Act 1984, applies only to dispositions by close companies (see p.81). By S.94 such dispositions are apportioned among the participators for the purpose of assessing them for inheritance tax. If the company is not a close company then the taxable disposition by each member who approves the transfer of bonus shares to the employee trust is the amount of the drop in value of their share-holding by reason of this settlement by the company.

Unless the settlement is very large this is likely to be small, especially as our articles provide for compulsory transfer of shares to be at par which should keep their value fairly constant unless a winding up, or sale, is imminent. If this exemption for employee trusts is not available the value attributable to each member for tax purposes may well come within the annual inheritance tax exemption, which currently stands at £3000. We have drawn the settlement so that it is exempt under S.58 from the periodic charge to tax on discretionary settlements. S.72 deals with tax on termination and appears to impose a charge on assets held on termination but not on payments made out of capital to persons other than those specified in sub-section (3), i.e. (a) persons who have provided any of the settled property otherwise than additions not exceeding £1000 in any one year, (b) five per cent participators and (c) persons who have bought an interest in the settled property.

Members' Capital Contribution

We have provided that members may make a certain minimum capital contribution, as shareholding, loan account or reserve account[14], a condition of membership. We have also suggested imposing an upper limit to this required contribution so that employees will not be barred from membership by a requirement for too high a capital contribution. In the case of a society the Registrar will probably require an upper limit. But we have included powers to allocate profits in such a way as to maintain desired levels of shareholding and loan and reserve accounts. In the case of societies we have also included a power to redeem shares in excess of the desired level. In the case of companies we have given power to refuse to issue shares, or approve transfers of shares, if that would result in a holding in excess of the desired level. The danger is that better off members may be tempted to seek control by fixing a high enough minimum to deter the lower paid from taking up membership. To assist the lower paid the minimum need not be a fixed sum but may be a sum representing so many months salary or average earnings. Also advice can be given on how to raise the money or the contribution can be accepted by instalments (probably with interest on the balance outstanding to make it fair for other members). The probability is that members will not be able to obtain all their capital requirements from outside sources and so will have to find some themselves, unless, perhaps, they have inherited large general reserves. Even in Mondragon, with support from their own bank, members have to make a substantial contribution.

14. See page 36.

OUTSIDE FINANCE

Short Term

Apart from any special borrowing facilities or government, or other, grants available in a particular case, the first port of call is likely to be a high street bank. Traditionally banks support businesses with overdraft facilities and fairly short term loans but circumstances vary so a discussion is always worthwhile. The bank's attitude will be similar to its attitude to other company applications. Its first concern will be the economic viability of the business as banks prefer successful rather than unsuccessful customers and do not want to encourage unpromising ventures.

The bank will then look for some available security, probably starting with freehold or leasehold premises. It will want to see that members are covering any initial losses and may ask for personal guarantees from members to cover at least part of the bank's indebtedness. But personal guarantees may not be asked for and even without security banks often support a promising business. If personal guarantees do become necessary then each member should make sure that the guarantee is limited to an amount which is not beyond the ability of that member to pay. If members' homes are charged then each member will want to be sure that even if the maximum amount of the guarantee has to be paid the house will not have to be sold. If possible members should give separate guarantees for part only of the total required rather than giving the usual joint and several guarantee for the whole, so that if 10 members are guaranteeing a £10,000 facility, each member should try to limit their own guarantee to £1000 rather than each member being liable for the full £10,000 (even though that member would have the right to obtain a contribution from the other guarantors.)

Longer Term Finance

For longer term outside finance the firm can approach merchant banks or other financial institutions which have money they want to invest. One of these is Industrial and Commercial Finance Corporation (ICFC)[15], a division of Investors in Industry plc, which specialises in support to small and medium sized businesses. It pioneered support for management buy-outs and so seems well placed to do the same for worker buy-outs if they should become popular. Up to 90% of the capital required is provided in a suitable case where the price is right and the prospects good. Most, if not all, is at fixed interest, either medium or long term loans or preference shares, but sometimes a

---

15. ICFC of 91 Waterloo Road, London SE1 8XP.

minority equity holding is required. The chance of a high return if the business prospers is demanded in exchange for a greater than usual risk of loss by business failure. In the case of a society only loans are available as neither non-voting shares not equity shares with no limit to the dividend which can be paid are permitted. However, a company using our constitution could issue preference shares in the ordinary way, and a class of non-voting ordinary shares if the basis of profit sharing was agreed.

If any preference shares issued are redeemable, and are in fact redeemed, then it must be borne in mind that their nominal value, paid out of general reserves, must be carried to a capital redemption reserve account which may not be distributed to members. So, for example, if the money raised by the issue of the shares had been used to buy a property and then enough profits were saved up and used to redeem the preference shares and the property was sold, it would not be permissible to divide the proceeds amongst the members. A sum equal to the nominal value of the redeemed shares should have to be kept back and would then form part of the permanent capital of the company[16]. However, if the money had initially been raised on loan there would be no such problem, as the amount of the loan would never have formed part of the company's own capital. Preference shares are, therefore, more appropriate when it is desired to increase the company's capital.

A Type of Equity

If the financial institution insists on some equity, or ordinary, shares then the situation is more complicated than in the case of a conventional company. A company need have only one class of ordinary shares and can simply issue a minority holding, say 25%, to the institution which will then automatically share in the ups and downs of the company, both as to dividends and capital gains. However, a problem does arise in the case of a company, probably a family company, where the directors and the shareholders are virtually the same people. The minority shareholder runs the risk that the directors will pay themselves a disproportionate share of profits as directors fees and then declare either a very small dividend or none at all. A similar situation would arise if a worker-controlled company issued a class of non-voting ordinary shares to an investor, as the members could pay high salaries and bonuses to themselves rather than declare a dividend.

ICFC have overcome this difficulty by evolving a special class of ordinary share for use when they insist on a share of the equity,

16. See page 41.

which they call a Cumulative Convertible Participating Preferred Ordinary Share. It is cumulative in that a dividend entitlement of one year which is not declared and paid is carried forward to subsequent years. It is convertible to the other members' class of ordinary shares at the option of ICFC, which would normally be exercised if the company was being sold. It is participating and preferred in that it is entitled to a percentage of total net profits before tax and directors' remuneration in preference to the other ordinary shares and then, when the other shares have received an equivalent rate, it participates in any further dividends on the same basis as the other ordinary shares.

As an example, the holding might be £50,000 representing 25% of the total ordinary shareholding, and the preferred dividend entitlement might be 5% of net profits before tax and directors' fees. Net profits of £10,000 would produce a preferred dividend of £500 (5% of £10,000) which represents a dividend of 1% of the holding of £50,000. If the net profits were £1,000,000 the dividend would be 5% of £1,000,000, i.e., £50,000 representing a yield of 100% on the holding. If any further dividends were paid after the payment of directors' fees they would go to the other shareholders up to the same rate, 1% or 100% in the examples given, and then at an equal rate per cent. to both classes of ordinary shares.

There is no reason why a similar class of ordinary share could not be negotiated with a worker controlled company using our model memorandum and articles of association provided, of course, that the lending institution had sufficient confidence in the prospects of the business. As the share of profits constituting the preferred part of the dividend would be expected to be calculated before any payments were made to the members either by way of salary or profit distribution, it should be less than the typical 5% for conventional companies. The institution will want to secure a share of profits which will give them the rate of interest they currently expect from an investment in such a private firm, say 15%, and will calculate it from previous accounts of the company, if it is a going concern, and from forecasts.

It is not immediately apparent how any further participation could be calculated as the members may not declare any dividend on their shares. Nor will the entitlement to a share of residual assets on winding up take care of itself without special provision. With a conventional company if the financial institution takes 25% of the issued ordinary shares then automatically the other shareholders have taken up 75% and on a winding up their entitlement is in the same proportion. But our model provides for the allocation of profits and of surplus assets on winding up to go to members according to their participation or as they determine, so it will be necessary to cover the rights of the investors' shares explicitly. However, if both parties want to do a deal it should be possible to overcome these problems. The lending institution may want a proportion of ploughed back profits credited to a reserve account in its name or issued to it as bonus shares. The company may want the right to purchase the investor's shares after a period of years at a valuation on an agreed basis. As each occasion is a separate negotiation a variety of methods can be discussed.

Greater Need for External Finance

A worker controlled firm is likely to meet less of its needs for new capital investment from ploughed back profits than is a conventional company because its members will probably want a substantial repayment of capital on retirement. If members own investments, apart from an interest in pension and insurance funds, they are likely to prefer investments which can easily be sold. If this is so, worker-controlled firms will need to go to the capital market for injections of capital more often than will their conventional counterparts. It is often said that the difficulty in obtaining capital has been a limiting factor in the growth of the producer co-operative sector. If that is the case then we hope that our model constitution for a company limited by shares will help this obstacle to be surmounted.

MANAGEMENT STRUCTURE

Legal Standing of Committee or Board

Responsibility for day-to-day management is vested in the committee of a society or the board of directors of a company. Members of the committee and individual directors have legal responsibilities for seeing that the firm complies with the law. They are also accountable to the members who elected them and must follow any directions laid down at a general meeting. If they feel they cannot then they should resign unless they can persuade the general meeting to change the direction. If the members are not satisfied with their performance the members cannot take over management but can dismiss any or all of the committee or directors and appoint others in their place. This structure is written in to the Acts and it enables third parties to deal with the committee or board knowing that it has power to bind the firm and use the seal when required. But some members, if not all, will want more consultation and a bigger say in decision making than an occasional vote for committee or board or for their dismissal.

Accountability to Members

When the firm is small enough all the members are likely to be on the committee or board, so the problem will not arise. But when the firm is larger, particularly when there are specialist jobs including managerial ones, the members will have to decide how they wish to use the structure. They may elect predominantly non-managerial members to the committee or board who then agree policy and have the managers report progress and problems to them. Or they may find it more convenient to elect managers or members with a particular interest in, or aptitude for, management. In either case the committee or board will be responsible for business decisions relating to suppliers and customers, production, sales and finance. If they are not to get out of touch with the rest of the members they will have to find ways of keeping them in the picture and discussing those aspects which members want to discuss. When the firm is not too big, and the committee or board is fairly representative of all groups of members, informal reporting and discussion may be perfectly satisfactory. But the larger the firm the more likely it is to need formal arrangements and to borrow the best practices from conventional companies, e.g. setting up works committees and councils at all levels of the organisation. They may look the same but will operate in a different power structure, so if management will not listen or co-operate a majority of members can call for their dismissal. As mentioned previously, it has been suggested that this is an area in which trade unions could play a vital role.

Electing Committee or Board by Proportional Representation

The manner in which the committee or board informs and consults the other members is outside the constitution and is for the members to decide from time to time. We have included in the constitution the normal method of voting for the committee or board under which each member can vote for each nominee. This can result in a minority group never succeeding in getting their candidate elected and feeling that insufficient attention is given to their point of view in the daily running of the business. We have accordingly given an alternative clause in a footnote to the model rules providing for the election of the committee by proportional representation with single transferable vote in accordance with the rules of the Electoral Reform Society.

The Electoral Reform Society can be employed to conduct the

election or their leaflets and booklet with full instructions can be obtained from them at 6 Chancel Street, London SE1 0UX. Under their system each member no longer has one vote for every vacancy to be filled but has one vote only. As some candidates are likely to receive more than enough votes to elect them each member may give a choice of candidate in exercising their vote so that if the first choice does not need more votes then the second choice comes into play and so on. The system provides for apportioning a candidate's surplus votes to other candidates in proportion to all the second choices of those voting for the elected candidate. The big advantage of this system is that it enables minority groups which are big enough to justify representation on the committee or board to receive such representation if enough of them vote for their candidate.

Chapter 3

Conversions and Take-overs

PURCHASE OF AN EXISTING BUSINESS
Available Choices
The co-operators will need to decide whether the new firm is to be registered as a company or as a co-operative society. One important consideration will be the arrangements they have made to finance the purchase as societies are restricted in the amount and type of shares they can issue. Shareholding is limited to £10,000 unless the shareholder is itself a co-operative society when there is no limit, and neither ordinary shares taking a share of profits nor a special class of fixed interest share are permitted. So an outside financier of a society is likely to opt for a loan, and will have to unless it is a co-operative society, if the amount involved is large. But if the new firm is to be a company then the financier can make loans or take preference shares or a special class of ordinary shares or a mixture of the three.

They will also need to decide whether to buy the existing firm by buying all its shareholding or to buy the assets and goodwill. If the shares are bought there will need to be a reconstruction of the company to make it worker controlled. If the assets are bought a new company will be formed, leaving the old one to wind itself up.

Redundancy Payments
If the purchasers, or some of them, are employees of the existing firm and have been employed for two years or more, they will want to consider their entitlement to a redundancy payment. If the shares are being bought then there is no entitlement as there is no termination of employment, the firm, however reconstructed, remaining the same employer.

If the assets are bought care needs to be taken if the entitlement is not to be lost. The new worker controlled company will be a successor employer which takes over the business and if such a successor employer offers a new job before the old employment contract expires, which new job starts within four weeks, the entitlement will be lost. If securing redundancy payments is important the co-operators could purchase the assets and business as partners with an agreement to sell to the new worker controlled firm after the four week period. In the meantime the co-operators would have unlimited liability and would probably agree to share profits and losses in proportion to their previous or anticipated earnings.

Agreement to form a Worker Controlled Firm

The co-operators would be well advised to have a sufficiently clear-cut and binding agreement to go through with the conversion before the purchase, or they may find themselves co-operating with the purchase only to end up with less rights than they had anticipated. If shares are bought they may well be transferred to nominees who will have de facto control until the conversion is carried through, so the members need an agreement binding the nominees. If the assets are being bought an agreement is equally necessary unless the new firm has already been formed and is itself making the purchase, in spite of the loss of redundancy payments that will occasion.

Purchase of a Conventional Company and Conversion to a Worker Controlled Company

(a) Reorganisation of the Company

There will need to be a reconstruction of the company to make it worker controlled. The Articles of Association can be amended, or changed, by a special resolution requiring a 75% majority. The Memorandum is not always as easy to change, but it is probable that if any change is needed it will be to the Objects clause which can also be changed by a special resolution under S.4 of the Companies Act 1985. The clause may be changed only for limited purposes set out in the Act but if a resolution is passed then under S.5 the members or debenture holders challenging it must commence court proceedings within 21 days. This seems to open the door to any change, provided all the co-operators are in favour, as once the 21 days have elapsed and the change has been registered it cannot be challenged.

Although our model articles have been based on the 1985 Companies Act version of Table A the amendments have been extensive in order to adapt to worker control, so we suggest that, rather than amend the existing Articles of the bought company, new model articles are substituted. At the same time the objects clause in the memorandum could be changed to that in our model. When drafting the articles we have borne in mind, not only the requirements of a new company, but also those that arise on a re-organisation. In particular, we have provided that employee shares held by non-employees will cease to carry votes. This is to cover the possibility that the articles are changed without re-organising the shareholding at the same time, e.g., if the existing articles do not give power to make the desired re-organisation. If so, those holding surplus shares will need a prior agreement to have them converted to new shares, cash or loan stock.

If the shares rather than assets are to be bought, care must be taken to see that the desired end can be achieved. The purchase price will be reflected in the balance sheet of the company being bought by the nominal shareholding and reserve accounts plus or minus any variation in the value of assets above or below their book value and subject to the actual negotiation. If the co-operators and their backers are willing to leave the total purchase price in the company as share capital of one sort or another there is no problem. But if they want to convert part of the price to loans there are snags. The nominal value of the shares will usually have to remain in as share capital to avoid the complications of a reduction of capital, and the same applies to any premium, or share redemption, reserve accounts there may be. It is true that any general reserves which represent accumulated profits available for distribution could be paid out, (but they would then be taxed as dividends) or they could be transferred, in whole or in part, to members' reserve accounts. Also, in so far as the purchase price exceeds the nominal shareholding and reserve accounts (other than any re-valuation reserve), it is possible to effect a reduction of capital by the company itself buying some of the shares from the co-operators out of capital[1]. The company can borrow the purchase price from another source, thereby converting part of the original purchase price from shareholding to loan, but the purchase price itself must be paid when the shares are purchased (S.159(3) and S.162(2) of the Companies Act 1985).

(b) Re-allocation of Shares

We have included in the articles a wide power to issue investor shares which could include preference shares and a class of non-voting ordinary shares with special rights. If it is desired to issue redeemable shares whether preference or ordinary then, under S.160(3) of the 1985 Act, the terms and manner of redemption must be set out in the articles. We have also included the power in Table A for the company to buy its own shares under S.162 of the

1. See page 56.

1985 Act, and to make the purchase out of capital if it comes within the terms of S.171 of the same Act.

The first necessity is to convert sufficient ordinary shares into the special class of employee ordinary share which can be held only by employees. Each of the employees who signed the agreement to convert the company may have had transferred to them one or more ordinary shares which will be converted to employee ordinary shares. If the shares were transferred to nominees then one or more of the new employee ordinary shares should be transferred by the nominees to each such employee. Control of the company will then be vested in the employees who were party to the agreement. As soon as the reorganisation is complete any remaining, or new, employees can be issued with a share or shares. Of course, each employee must comply with the conditions of membership, including making any required loan to the company. If the authorised capital has already been fully issued and is fully paid then in the case of a private company it may be convenient to retain a fairly nominal holding of ordinary shares in the name of a nominee to hold on behalf of the company so that they can be transferred to new employees as required. In the meantime, as they have been converted to employee ordinary shares, they cease to carry votes as voting rights are restricted to employees.

All the remaining ordinary shares must then be converted either into preference shares or non-voting ordinary shares with special rights, according to the arrangements made with those financing the purchase. If an existing issue of preference shares was also bought it may be desired to convert it to a new issue with different rights. The nominal value of any new issue to replace ordinary shares, and perhaps preference shares, will have to be agreed in advance as, unless the purchase price happens to be equal to the nominal value, some adjustment will have to be made. The nominal value of the new issue will have to equal or exceed that of the existing issue as an issue at a lower figure would amount to a reduction of capital. If the price paid for the shares is less than the nominal value then the rate of interest can be appropriately less than the agreed rate of return on the money invested. If 1,000 £1 shares were bought for £750 and the agreed rate of return was 10%, i.e., £75 p.a., then an issue of 1,000 shares at 7½% would produce the desired income. The preferential participation in a winding up, at £1,000 or £750 or some other figure, would also have to be specified.

If the price paid for the shares is more than the nominal value then a similar adjustment could be made to the rate of interest. If 1,000 £1 shares were bought for £1,250 then an interest rate of

12½% would produce a return of 10% on the money invested. Provision could also be made that on a winding up the preference shareholders should receive 125% before the ordinary shareholders receive anything. From the investor's point of view it is like any other purchase of a fixed interest share above par or taking up new shares at a premium. However, if a premium is paid, the amount has to be carried to a share premium reserve and cannot be paid out in dividends. But in the case of a purchase there is, of course, no such requirement that the price paid will be reflected in the share and premium accounts in the balance sheet, but a probability that it will be reflected partly in reserve accounts including revaluation reserves. As these reserve accounts can be used for the benefit of the employee members the investors may want their investment to be shown, as far as possible, on the balance sheet as share capital. In that case they can ask for an issue of bonus shares out of any reserves which are available for this purpose, i.e., share premium and capital redemption reserves and reserves which represent profits available for distribution. If this still leaves an unacceptable shortfall the company could buy the shares, under the powers mentioned below, partly out of capital, paying for them by an issue of shares to take up existing capital and available reserves, and the balance left on loan or covered by loan stock.

If some of the ordinary shares are to be converted to a new issue of investor's non-voting ordinary shares with special rights, then the rights must be fully set out either in the articles of association or in a special resolution which is then permanently attached to the articles. The matters to be covered include share of profits, any entitlement to bonus issues out of reserves and any option to purchase to be given to the company.

(c) Purchase by the Company of its own shares

The re-organisation of share capital can also be carried out by the company exercising the power to purchase its own shares contained in S.162 of the Companies Act 1985, although the tax effect should always be given careful consideration[2]. It is necessary that the articles of association contain this power which is in Table A and which we have included in our model. The purchased shares have to be cancelled but this does not operate

---

2. The treatment for tax will depend on whether the payment made by the company for the shares counts as a distribution as defined in the Taxes Act 1970 Part X as amended by the Finance Act 1972 Schedule 22. In brief, the payment for the shares will not count as a distribution in so far as it is a repayment of capital, i.e., does not exceed the amount paid on the issues of the shares, but any excess is a distribution.

as a reduction of authorised capital[3]. The shares may be paid for by an issue of new shares or by cash or partly one and partly the other. So the people financing the purchase can take shares or cash as agreed and any cash taken can be lent to the new company.

With the one exception mentioned in the next paragraph, the nominal value of the purchased shares must remain in the company's balance sheet as part of the company's capital, either as a new issue of shares or as a credit to the share redemption reserve[4]. If it were not for this provision then a company could buy its own shares as a simple way to reduce capital without the supervision of the court. So, if the price for the shares is a new issue of shares of a lower nominal value than the shares purchased then the difference must be carried to the capital redemption reserve. An issue of shares of a higher nominal value than the shares being purchased is possible only if there are sufficient profits available for distribution to issue as bonus shares, as otherwise the new issue would be tantamount to making an issue at a discount. If the price paid is cash, then it must come from profits available for distribution or from capital under the new powers discussed in the next paragraph. If the whole payment is made from profits available for distribution the nominal value of the shares purchased must be carried to the capital redemption reserve. If it is partly in cash from profits available for distribution and partly from a new issue of shares then the amount to be carried to the capital redemption reserve is the amount by which the nominal value of the shares purchased exceeds the amount of the new issue.

The one case when the purchase by a company of its own shares can be from capital and thereby effect a reduction of capital without going to court is under the provisions of S.171 of the Companies Act 1985. This power is available only to private companies and only when there are insufficient profits available for distribution to meet the price after taking account of any new issue made for the purpose. This provision would cover the situation where the company purchased has little or no profits carried forward but a valuable property showing a very substantial unrealised profit over its purchase price. If those financing the purchase want their investment to be by way of loan then the surplus ordinary shares and all preference shares can be bought by the company with the purchase money left outstanding as loans to the company. If they want to take shares as well as leaving money in as loans then shares can be issued up

3. Companies Act 1985 S.160 (4).
4. Companies Act 1985 S.170.

to an amount not exceeding the nominal value of the purchased shares plus any profits available for distribution and the balance left as loans. Any profits available for distribution have to be used first and the nominal value of the shares purchased less the payment out of capital has to be taken to the capital redemption reserve[5]. If the whole payment is made out of capital, there being no profits available for distribution, the amount by which the nominal value exceeds the payment out of capital must be taken to the capital redemption reserve. But the payment out of capital is, in effect, financed by the re-valuation reserve.

A private company may buy its shares out of capital only if it has power to do so under its articles so we have included the power given in Table A. Also it has to complete the procedure set out in S.174 of the Act which includes a tight time schedule. The directors have to make a statutory declaration that the payment out of capital is a permissible capital payment under the Act, that, when made, the company will be able to pay its debts and will be able to carry on business as a going concern and pay its debts as they fall due throughout the ensuing year. This declaration will have to be approved by the auditors in advance as their report, broadly in support of the directors' view, must be available with the statutory declaration of the directors at the meeting of shareholders which approves the payment by special resolution. This special resolution must be passed on, or within one week after, the date of the statutory declaration. The payment must then be made not less than five nor more than seven weeks after the date of the resolution and must be publicised.

Purchase of a Conventional Company and Conversion to an Industrial and Provident Societies Act Society

If the purchasers wish to convert the company to an I & P S Act society they and their financial backers can buy the company's shares between them and can then use the procedure set out in S.53 of the I & P S Act 1965. A special resolution is passed deciding to convert to a society with rules already drawn up and identified and seven persons are authorised to sign the rules with the secretary, which rules are then lodged with the Registrar of Friendly Societies. After the rules are approved by the Registrar he provides a certificate that the rules have been registered, which certificate together with a copy of the special resolution are lodged with the Registrar of Companies and upon his registering the resolution and certificate the conversion takes effect and the

5. Companies Act 1985 S.171.
6. I&PS Act 1965 Schedule I.

registrar cancels the registration under the Companies Acts.

The special resolution should either authorise the seven signatories to the rules to agree any alterations suggested by the Registrar or require them to lay any such alterations before a general meeting for their decision. The resolution may also provide for the conversion of any shares over the statutory limit for societies into transferable loan stock with such interest as may be fixed and repayable on such conditions as are determined in the resolution. The Act refers only to the conversion of shares over the statutory limit so if it is desired to specify a lower limit, as in ICOM model rules, the rules approved by special resolution should contain a provision for converting such further shares as may be desired into loan stock or for the repayment of such shares. We have covered this situation in rules numbered 10 and 11.

If the company's shares are not bought at par then some problems will have to be sorted out. If the shares are below par it is probably because the business is worth less than the nominal value of the shareholding. In that case it is not possible to repay all the shareholding or convert too many shares into loans without making the society insolvent. However, if a substantial conversion of shares to loans is desired, it would be quite possible for all the members to release a proportion of their loans so that the total of their shares and loans was more nearly equivalent to the price they paid. If there is no substantial conversion of shares to loans then the only danger would be if too many shares were redeemed at par. We have covered this in rule 10 by providing for the redemption of shares at an auditor's valuation when this is below par.

If the shares are bought above par than the purchasing members will have paid to the previous shareholders more than their total of new shares and loans which they may not find satisfactory. The members may be content to adopt a policy of issuing new shares out of profits to bring their shareholding up to the purchase price as soon as possible. In that case, an immediate start might be made by issuing shares out of reserves which represent accumulated profits carried forward. If not issued as shares, some of the reserves can be carried to the members' reserve accounts and re-valuation reserves can also be credited to members. A financial backer may well want to make loans rather than take shares in which case the loans can be to the members in the first place. The members then buy the shares, part of which are converted to loan stock, which is then transferred to the financial backer in repayment of its loans to the individual members.

Purchase of a Society and Conversion to a Worker Controlled Society or Companies Act Company

It may be unlikely that one set of co-operators will want to buy out another set but it could happen. Perhaps more likely is a situation where the working members of a traditional co-operative want to buy out the non-working members. In either case the rules should be checked to see what is provided for the transferability of shares, which is one of the things which have to be covered in the rules[6]. If the shares can be transferred it is then necessary to see that the desired transfers will not give anyone more than the maximum holding, which could easily happen if the number of buyers was less than the number of sellers. If this is a problem the sellers can be asked to convert some shares to loans or to agree to redeem a proportion of the shareholding on or before completion which may well require borrowing organised by the purchasers.

If the new co-operative is to be carried on as a society this can be achieved by a change of the rules. Provision for altering the rules is another item which has to be specified in the rules[6] so they should be consulted. The change can be effected by substituting a new set of rules for the old. No change takes effect until registered and the fee for changing to new rules which are model rules is £100 or to non-model rules is £220. This compares with the fee on registering a new society which is £140 if model rules are used and £330 if not. Our draft rules are not "model" for this purpose and will only become so if arrangements are made with a sponsoring organisation to have them agreed with the Registrar of Friendly Societies as "model rules".

If the new worker-controlled business is to be carried on as a company, use can be made of the procedure set out in S.52 of the I & P S Act 1965. A special resolution is required which must be passed by a three fourths majority at one general meeting and then passed again by a simple majority at a second general meeting held not less than fourteen days nor more than a month after the first. The Act provides that if the resolution contains the particulars required by the Companies Acts to be contained in the memorandum of association then a sealed copy issued by the Registrar of Companies has the same effect as a memorandum duly signed and attested under the Companies Acts. In practice it will be desirable to adopt new articles of association as well as the memorandum at the meetings so that they can both be registered at the same time. Once registered with the Registrar of Companies the registration under the I & P S Acts becomes void and is cancelled.

6. I & PS Act 1965 Schedue 1.

In either case if the shares are bought at more or less than their nominal value the problems mentioned above will arise. If they are below par then the firm is unlikely to be able to afford to redeem too many shares at par. Members may wish to surrender a proportion of their shares or rely on a provision, such as that contained in our rules, permitting redemption at a valuation when this is less than par. If the price paid was above par then on death or retirement the member or the member's personal representatives may receive less than was paid for the shares. In that case issuing new shares, converting shares to loans or crediting loan or reserve accounts, as explained on page 58, may be available. Any such action should be carried out before conversion to a company because once this is done the share capital becomes locked in as capital and the options are immediately restricted to those discussed above. If our model memorandum and articles are used then before conversion, if a desired level of shareholding has been decided upon, any member's holding which is above it should be reduced to that level so that on conversion the holding will be changed to the special class of employee controlling shares and there will be no surplus shares to be got rid of. The reduction can be achieved by converting the surplus shares to loans, if necessary by redeeming the shares, if permitted by the rules, and borrowing back the redemption money.

Purchase of the Assets and Goodwill of the Existing Business

It may be that only the assets and goodwill are on the market. Perhaps the business is being bought from a sole proprietor or a partnership, or a company is selling off part only of its undertaking. But there may well be a choice, in which case the vendors are likely to favour one course rather than the other because the incidence of tax is likely to be different and so may demand a higher price for the less favoured option. The co-operators also will have to consider the tax implications since the rules for assessing tax on a new business, as well as on a closing business, are different from those which apply to a continuing business. Also, the company may have carried forward losses which can be set off against future profits for tax purposes. The tax implications are complex so the co-operators would do well to consult their accountants if they have any choice in the matter. Presumably they will, in any event, be asking their accountants to advise on the state and health of the business as disclosed in the accounts.

There are two other, perhaps more fundamental, aspects which may rule out a purchase of shares if a purchase of assets can be negotiated. It may be that the co-operators want to carry on as a company with a small share capital, relying on borrowing for finance, and there is no way that the existing share capital can be reduced to an acceptable level. Or it may be that securing redundancy payments for those co-operators already working for the company is essential, in which case they must become self-employed partners for a period as discussed earlier. If the vendors will only sell the shares it may be necessary to buy them and then, as controllers of the company, direct it to sell the assets to themselves as partners[7]. The purchase price of the assets can be left outstanding and set off against the amount due to the members on the winding up of the company which is immediately put in hand. The new company or society is then formed, either immediately or after four weeks self-employment if redundancy payments are being secured, and it buys the business from the members. The money put up to buy the shares of the original company then becomes shares in, or loans to, the new co-operative firm. Additional expense and stamp duty will probably be involved and if there is a substantial capital gain on the sale of the assets to the workers corporation tax on the chargeable gain could be prohibitive. Indeed, this could be the reason why the vendors themselves refused to sell the assets.

SALE OF A WORKER-CONTROLLED FIRM AND CONVERSION TO A CONVENTIONAL COMPANY

The fact that a business is worker-controlled does not prevent it from being the subject of a take-over bid but does prevent it taking place unless at least 75% of the employees are in favour. In both constitutions in this book employee members have control on the basis of one person one vote so the normal method of take-over, i.e., buying a majority of shares, does not apply. Instead, if the purchasers want control by capital, they will have to secure conversion to a conventional company unless they buy the assets and goodwill leaving the worker-controlled firm to wind up. But there may well be compelling tax or other reasons for preferring a sale of shares. If the business is small and the purchasers themselves will be the main employees, they can buy the shares and then convert to a conventional company. Otherwise they will need to insist that the conversion is carried out by the existing members. The procedure for conversion of an I&PS Act society to a company has been outlined above. If the worker-controlled firm is already registered as a company then the memorandum and articles can be amended in the same way as on a conversion from conventional company to worker control, also outlined above.

7. So long as their number does not exceed 20.

The co-operators may have received an offer which they feel is too good to refuse or they may have already decided to put the business on the market. They may have met some intractable problem such as the need for more capital than they are able or willing to raise. Some or all of them may remain as employees after the conversion. Whatever happens there will be a need to agree the apportionment amongst themselves of the purchase price. If it exceeds the nominal value of the shareholding then the members will probably expect the same sort of distribution as would have taken place on a winding up. As members' entitlement under our constitution is according to participation rather than shareholding, but the purchasers will be making an offer for shares, it will be necessary to adjust each member's entitlement before the sale.

Our constitutions give wide powers to the members in general meeting to adopt a policy with regard to the desired level of members' shareholdings and loan and reserve accounts. Also profits, which include undistributed profits from earlier years, may be allocated to members as bonus payments either as cash, bonus shares or credits to loan accounts. With these powers it ought to be possible to adjust each member's shareholding and other entitlements as may be agreed by the members, or at least by 75% of them. Of course without a 75% majority there can be no valid resolution either to wind up or to convert to a conventional company.

Chapter 4

Gift of a Conventional Company to the Employees

Inheritance Tax Exemption and Capital Gains Tax Roll Over Relief

There may be occasions when the owners of a family company have no one in the family wishing to carry on the business and prefer to give, or sell it at an undervalue, to the work-force rather than see it disbanded or swallowed up by a larger concern. If so they will probably want to take advantage of the exemption from inheritance tax contained in the Inheritance Tax Act 1984 and the roll-over relief from capital gains tax contained in Section 149 of the Capital Gains Tax Act 1979. These reliefs are available only if the gift, or gift element if there is a sale at an undervalue, is made to an employee trust which meets the qualifications set out in Section 86. There is the further advantage that once the trust is set up it is exempt from the inheritance tax discretionary trust regime both as to tax every ten years and on payments out to a qualifying beneficiary.[1]

These exemptions are given both to a settlement of shares in the company by the shareholders and a settlement of money or assets by a close company.[2] Different conditions apply to each but some common criteria apply and the employee trust must comply with Section 86. The trusts may not permit the settled property to be applied otherwise than for the benefit of:

(a) persons of a class defined by reference to employment in a particular trade or profession or employment by, or office with, a body carrying on a trade, profession or undertaking; or

(b) persons of a class defined by reference to marriage or relationship to, or dependence on, persons of a class defined as in (a) above;

---

1. Inheritance Tax Act 1984 Ss.58 and 72. The exemption is lost if the beneficiary has provided any of the settled property, other than additions not exceeding £1000 in any one year of assessment.
2. By Ss.28 and 13 respectively.

but if for the benefit of such persons then charitable purposes may also be included.

If the beneficiaries are defined by reference to employment by or office with a particular body, then:

(a) the class must comprise all or most of the persons employed or holding office with the body; or

(b) be held on the trusts of an approved profit sharing scheme.[3]

However there must be excluded from the class of beneficiaries for whose benefit any of the settled property may be applied at any time (subject to the exceptions mentioned below):

(a) A participator in the company as defined in Chapter III of Part XI of the Taxes Act 1970 other than a person who would be a participator only by reason of being a loan creditor. These are briefly persons who:

(1) possess or are entitled to acquire share capital or voting rights,

(2) possess or are entitled to acquire a right to receive or participate in distributions of the company or any amounts payable by the company to loan creditors by way of premium on redemption,

(3) are entitled to secure that income or assets (present or future) will be applied directly or indirectly for their benefit.

(b) A participator in any close company that has made a disposition of property to the same settlement to which Section 13 applies.

(c) A person who has been a participator in the company or a company referred to in (b) above at any time after or during the ten years before the transfer.

(d) Any person who is connected with any of the above mentioned participators. By virtue of Section 270 of the Inheritance Tax Act 1984 and Section 63 of the Capital Gains Tax Act 1979 the class of persons treated as connected with the participator will include the following:

(1) his or her spouse

(2) any brother sister ancestor or lineal descendant of the participator or his or her spouse

(3) any uncle aunt nephew or niece of the participator or of his or her spouse

(4) any spouse of a person mentioned in (2) or (3) above

(5) any trustee of a settlement of which the participator is "settlor" as defined by Section 44 of the Inheritance Tax Act 1984.

3. Approval in accordance with Schedule 9 to the the FA 1978.

The exemptions are:

(a) Participators in a company mentioned above do not include a participator who:

(1) is not beneficially entitled to, or to rights entitling him to acquire, 5% or more of, or of any class of, the shares comprised in its issued share capital; and

(2) on a winding up of the company would not be entitled to 5% or more of its assets.

(b) In determining whether the trusts permit property to be applied for the benefit of any beneficiary no account shall be taken of any power to make a payment which is income of such person for any of the purposes of income tax.

In the case of a settlement of shares, S.28 provides the further qualification that at the date of transfer or within one year thereafter:

(a) The Trustees must

(1) hold more than half of the ordinary shares in the company; and

(2) have a majority vote on all questions affecting the company as a whole. But this latter requirement does not apply to the question of winding up the company or questions primarily affecting shares or securities of a particular class if the company has shares or securities of that class with powers of voting limited to either or both of those questions.

(b) There are no provisions in any agreement or instrument affecting the company's constitution or management whereby the conditions in (a) above can cease to be satisfied without the consent of the trustees.

The combined effect of Section 28 and Section 86 is to exempt the gift to the trustees from tax and also exempt the trust from inheritance tax while it lasts and on certain payments out but not on termination.[4] But to secure this advantage there are three main conditions. First, all or most of the employees must be included, but there must be excluded anyone with a 5% or greater interest in the company. Secondly, within a year control of the company must pass to the trustees. And, thirdly, there must be no prior agreement or arrangement whereby this control can be taken away without the consent of the trustees. However, there is nothing to stop the settlor or settlors appointing themselves trustees so that they will have a guiding hand in how the trust is administered.

In the case of a settlement of money or assets by the company itself under Section 13 there is no requirement that control of the

---

4. See note 1 above.

company shall pass to the trustees. But, nevertheless, such a settlement can be used to hand over control by the company settling sufficient cash to enable the trustees to buy enough shares to get control. The shareholders' agreement should be obtained to the settlement and it might be necessary to amend the Memorandum or Articles of Association to give power to make the settlement. If substantial sums are settled by the company, then its assets value, and so the value of its shares, will be reduced. If the shareholders wish to increase the gift element by selling at an undervalue, then they will have to make sure that the trustees will obtain control and that the other conditions of a settlement of shares are met. If the owners want to dispose of the business but retain the company then the company can transfer its assets to the trustees, who can sell the assets to a new company formed by the employees in exchange for an issue of shares or loan stock.

The Period and Terms of the Trust

The gift to the employees by way of a trust, as opposed to an outright gift of shares to individual employees, might well be to secure the tax advantages outlined above. On the other hand it is very probable that the donors want to secure that the employees can continue the business rather than take a cash gift by selling their shares to the highest bidder. For this reason they may well specify a minimum period before the capital can be handed over to the beneficiaries. A maximum period is laid down by law in the rule against perpetuities, which is a fixed period not exceeding 80 years specified in the trust deed, or a life or lives in being at the date of the deed plus 21 years thereafter[5]. The trust deed may provide for the termination of the trusts at the end of a specified period or on the happening of an event, e.g. on the winding up of the company. Or it may give the trustees power to terminate the trusts and distribute the capital amongst the beneficiaries either at any time or after a minimum period of after the happening of an event.

In the meantime the trustees will receive such dividends as are paid on their shares and will apply them for the benefit of the beneficiaries in their discretion, or as laid down in the trust deed. As owners of all, or a majority, of the ordinary shares they will appoint the directors and have the last word on most policy matters. Although they cannot declare a larger dividend than they can persuade the directors to recommend, they can refuse to declare any dividend or limit it to a figure of their choosing. They can build up reserves, thereby increasing the value of their shares

5. The Perpetuities and Accumulations Act 1964, s.1.

and the capital in the trust, if they think that that is in the best interests of the beneficiaries. On the other hand they could pay out the maximum dividends the company can afford and they could initiate a policy of putting some reserves to employee's reserve accounts or otherwise provisionally crediting employees with a share in the reserves. Although the donors may well count on the continuation of the trust as a means of avoiding a sale or winding up and distribution of the capital, they may want the employees to assume control of, or have a large say in, the running of the business. Indeed, there might be a difficulty in finding trustees who are willing to take on the responsibility of controlling a business. The donor or donors could appoint themselves trustees and in our model deed we have given them the power to appoint new trustees as an alternative to the statutory power of trustees to appoint their successors.

The John Lewis Partnership and the Scott Bader Commonwealth are two well known examples of a successful business being handed over to trustees with control passing to the workforce who also receive a substantial share of profits. The John Lewis Partnership was established by two settlements, the first made in 1929 and the second in 1950. They continue until the expiration of 21 years from the death of the last survivor of the issue of King Edward VII who were alive on the 18th April 1927 or on all the Partnership companies ceasing to trade. The dividends on the settled shares, which include a controlling interest in the ordinary shares, are paid to the employees as a bonus in proportion to earnings in the previous year. The accounts to the 29th January 1983 show accumulated profits and other retentions at £273,411,000 and the number of employees at 28,200. At the end of the trust period the controlling ordinary shares which were settled in 1950 go as may be appointed by the trustee, or in default of appointment, to charity. The trustee is the John Lewis Partnership Trust Ltd., a company created for the purpose. The provisions for controlling the business are complicated and are contained partly in the 1950 Settlement and partly in the constitution. The constitution provides for a central council up to one fifth members nominated by the chairman of the company, who is also chairman of the Trust Company, the remainder being elected by all the employees. Power is shared between the council and the chairman who appoints his deputy and his successor. The chairman and the council each nominate five directors so the balance of power seems to be with the chairman but, nevertheless, he can be removed by a two thirds majority of the council.[6]

According to their booklet *Scott Bader*, published in 1973, the shares in the trading company are all owned by Scott Bader Commonwealth Ltd. which is a registered charity. The duration of the trust is not mentioned, but as charities are not bound by the rule against perpetuities it could be indefinite. As the trusts are charitable one assumes that the capital will never be handed over to the employees, but they are given substantial control and a right to share in profits. The constitution provides that a minimum of 60% of profits must be ploughed back for consolidation, taxation and reserves, leaving a maximum of 40% for distribution. Of the distributed profits as much must go to charity as goes to members by way of bonus. It is said that bonuses are distributed equally rather than in proportion to salary. Subject to the limitations imposed by the constitution the employees appear to have control of the trust company, Scott Bader Commonwealth Ltd., which is a company limited by guarantee. Membership is limited to employees of the trading company, Scott Bader Company Ltd., over 18 who have been with the company for at least 12 months and each member has one vote.[7]

As our concern is with worker control we have not explored ways of sharing, or limiting, that control on the lines of the John Lewis Partnership or the Scott Bader Commonwealth. Also, we have assumed a distribution of capital to the employees in some form and at some stage as the probable conclusion of the trust. As explained, in order to get the tax reliefs mentioned, the trustees must start with the right to administer the trusts as they see fit. If the employees already have a democratic constitution, comprising a works council or hierarchy of works councils or similar bodies, there is no reason why the trustees should not consult them and seek their advice. If there is no such constitution, they can still consult the employees individually and encourage them to set up a democratic constitution. It may well be that this is how the settlors consider that the company should be run, at least for a period. But sooner or later the capital will have to be handed over to the beneficiaries and, rather than distribute the shares amongst them, we have given the trustees two options to hand over collectively, such options to come into effect at whatever date may be specified in the trust deed.

One option is to hand over control, including the power to

6. The John Lewis Partnership kindly made available to us their printed book containing their Constitution, copy settlements, Court Orders and Memorandum and Articles of Association of their trust company (John Lewis Partnership Trust Ltd.).
7. Taken from their publication *Scott Bader* 1973, giving a brief account of the Company and the formation and operation of the Commonwealth (Scott Bader Commonwealth Ltd.).

distribute capital, to an employees' organisation. We have provided that the trustees have to be satisfied that its rules make it a substantially democratic organisation on the basis, in general, of one person one vote; that the beneficiaries under the trust who are also employees of the company, i.e., not ex-employees or dependants, are all members, and the only members, of the employees' organisation; and that a 75% majority vote of the organisation is required for a resolution to wind up the organisation or to use any voting rights it may have in the company to support a special resolution of the company. We have included this power as a means of terminating the trust so it is imperative that it constitutes a disposal of the capital to beneficiaries authorised by the trust deed. So, not only must the organisation be limited to beneficiaries, but also they must have power under their rules to divide up the capital amongst themselves or amongst themselves and any other beneficiaries under the trust deed. Unless and until divided the capital would remain in the hands of the trustees, or of the new trustees appointed for the purpose, but they would then be nominees of the organisation and the terms of the trust deed would cease to apply. The settlors may well wish to delay the time when the employees can distribute capital for as long as possible so we have put in a further provision to facilitate control by the employees and retention of the capital by the trustees. This is a power for the trustees to delegate any of their powers and discretions for one or more fixed periods to an employees' organisation whose rules meet the criteria set out above. Such an employees' organisation would resemble that set up under the Constitution of the John Lewis Partnership but without the special powers of the chairman. But the roles are different, as in the Partnership the Council has constitutional power of control, but no power to dispose of capital, whereas under our scheme the trustees either give the organisation an advisory role with or without delegating some powers to them for limited periods, or hand over complete power, including the right to distribute capital.

The other option included in our model deed arises out of the powers to re-organise the company and to transfer assets, including shares, to beneficiaries. This has the effect of allowing, but not requiring, the trustees to convert the company into a worker-controlled one, on the lines of our model. In that case each employee beneficiary will receive one or more shares of the special class of controlling share reserved for employees, and once again, it is essential that only qualifying beneficiaries should be included. The remaining shares will be converted to preference shares with whatever rights to dividend and on winding up as are decided by the trustees. The trustees may require very little in the way of dividends but by retaining a capital stake in the company they can influence the future of the company provided the settlement has given them power to appoint capital to charity rather than to employees. In that case if, in the opinion of the trustees, the employee members are proposing to wind up or sell prematurely the trustees can intimate that they are likely to exercise that power and distribute the capital, represented by the preference shares, to charity. If the trustees hold assets, rather than shares, they can achieve the same result by selling the assets to a new worker-controlled company in exchange for an issue of preference shares, or loan stock if that is preferred. By converting their ordinary shares or assets to preference shares or loan stock the trustees fix the capital in money terms so that any appreciation in value goes automatically to the employee members as controlling shareholders. The conversion to worker-control will constitute a partial distribution of capital if the value of the preference shares retained by the trustees is less than the value of the ordinary shares they surrendered. It is important, therefore, that the employees who receive new ordinary shares from the trustees all qualify as beneficiaries under the trust deed. From then on the only property subject to the trusts is the holding of preference shares or loan stock. Eventually it, too, will be transferred to beneficiaries. However, on the first transfer to beneficiaries, care must be taken not to make them five per cent participators and therefore excluded persons under the terms of the settlement or they will not qualify for any further distributions of capital. Therefore, in the case of small companies, it may be necessary to divest all the capital to the employee members or their employee's organisation in one go before they have become five per cent participators.

Chapter 5

Income and Corporation Tax

Corporation Tax

From the 1st April 1985 the rate of corporation tax is the same for societies as for companies. Societies had previously been taxed at a special rate of 40% which was less than the then rate of corporation tax on large companies of 50%. For the 1986 financial year the small companies rate was 29% for companies with profits of no more than £100,000. The standard rate of 35% is charged on profits in excess of £500,000. The relevant legislation provides for tapering relief on company profits falling between these two markers.

Interest paid on shares in a society receive special treatment under S. 340 of the Taxes Act 1970 which allows the interest to be deducted before computing corporation tax. This is in contrast to dividends on shares in a company which are not deductible although the advance corporation tax may be set off against the company's liability to mainstream corporation tax. As the advance corporation tax can be set off from the dividend this means that the company finishes up paying the difference between the rate of advance corporation tax, which is the same as basic rate income tax, and the rate of corporation tax paid by the company. At present only larger companies suffer now that the small companies rate of corporation tax is the same as the basic rate of income tax.

Salaries and any bonus paid should all be good deductions in computing profits for tax. However, there is a condition laid down in S. 130(a) of the Taxes Act 1970 that the payment must be made wholly and exclusively for the purposes of the trade, profession or vocation and the Revenue do from time to time successfully challenge payments to directors as being so out of proportion to the contribution of the director as to fail to pass this test. The firm may decide how much to pay but the Commissioners of Taxes will decide how much of it was paid for the purposes of the business in the assessment of corporation tax.

It seems to be open to the Revenue to make the same challenge to profits distributed to members as a bonus if they are very high and out of proportion to the member's contribution.

If there is an employee trust then dividends may well be paid to the trustees for the benefit of members or other beneficiaries in which case they will not be a good deduction for corporation tax purposes. If the small companies rate is paid this hardly matters, but if the standard rate is paid it should be possible to restrict dividends to the amount required by non-member beneficiaries. Other sums required by members should be paid directly to them as bonuses. With this in mind it might be desired to make the dividend on any preference shares issued to trustees of an employee trust non-cumulative, so that the full dividend is paid only if required by the trustees. Of course there is then the risk that the company will pay less than the trustees want.

Members' Loan Accounts and Members' Reserve Accounts

Under our constitutions any profits credited to employee members' loan accounts are part of distributed profits and so will be treated for tax in the same way as if they had been paid out to the member and then lent back to the firm. It is a good deduction in computing the firm's corporation tax, but it is assessed to tax as part of the member's income.

But any sums credited to members' reserve accounts remain part of the firm's reserves and a general meeting has power to transfer them to general reserves at any time. Such credits never belong to the member and so are not taxed as part of the member's income. Therefore they are not a good deduction in computing the firm's corporation tax any more than are credits to any other reserve account.

Lump Sum Payments and Pensions on Retirement

The repayment of a member's loan account, or, in the case of a society, share account as well, will not give rise to any tax consequences unless the shares are repaid below par when there will be a loss for capital gains tax purposes. But payment to members of part or the whole of their reserve accounts is subject to the same tax provisions as any other golden handshake. The treatment will depend on whether or not the members have a contractual right to the payment. If they have, then the members will pay income tax on them as emoluments of their employment. If they have no contractual right, then they will come within the provisions of Secs. 187 and 188 of the Taxes Act 1970 as amended by the Finance Act 1981 S. 31 and the Finance Act 1982 S. 43 which apply only if the payments are not otherwise chargeable to tax, e.g., voluntary payments or damages for breach of certain contractual rights. These sections exempt the first £25,000 and contain special rules for taxing the excess. Members will want to secure this substantial tax concession but, on the other hand, may not be as willing to build up large reserve accounts to help the business grow unless they feel confident that their share will be returned to them. We have provided an alternative clause in our model rules, but not articles, as explained on p.37. Whether the payments are voluntary or contractual they will be good deductions for corporation tax purposes provided that they, like other payments to members mentioned above, are made wholly and exclusively for the purposes of the trade. Any reasonable scheme to encourage employees and secure their co-operation in the enterprise should pass the test.

Another tax effective way of making provision for members on retirement is to participate in, or set up, an exempt approved pension scheme. Approval to the scheme must be obtained from the Inland Revenue Superannuation Funds Office (SFO) [1] who will supply details of their requirements. Contributions by the firm are allowable deductions for corporation tax purposes and contributions from members as employees are free of income tax up to 15% of remuneration. The fund itself is largely exempt from income tax and capital gains tax and so is a very favourable form of investment. The pension to be provided is limited to two thirds of final pensionable salary after 10 years employment if retirement is at normal retirement age. The scheme may allow part of the pension to be commuted, may provide a tax free lump sum if the member dies in employment and make provision for widows and dependants.

The pension fund can be managed by an insurance company or other outside organisation or be self-administered by trustees appointed by the firm, at least one of whom will have to be a professional person approved by the SFO. If the scheme is self-administered and the firm is a company with shares available for investors then there is the possibility of the trustees investing part of the pension funds, but not exceeding 50%, in the company itself. This could be an alternative to an employee trust as a means of capitalising some reserves in a way that is beneficial to members. Such an arrangement would have the advantage over the issue of bonus shares to an employee trust in that the company's contribution to the pension fund would be tax deductible without increasing the employee's taxable

1. The address of the Inland Revenue Superannuation Funds Office is Apex Tower, High Street, New Malden, Surrey, KT3 4DN.

emoluments whereas bonus issues can only be made out of profits which have already borne corporation tax.

Profit Sharing Schemes

Part III of the Finance Act 1978 gave tax concessions to profit sharing schemes which had been approved by the Revenue under the provisions set out in schedule 9 of that Act and since then the Act has been amended by the Finance Acts of 1980, '82, '85 and '86. The company gives money to the trustees of the scheme who use it to buy, or take up, shares in the company which they then allocate to individual employees, although they are kept in the trustees' names. The scheme must include all directors and employees who have served for a qualifying period not exceeding five years. Although allocated to individual employees the shares must not be sold for a retention period of two years and if then sold before the release date three years later the employees will lose a proportion of their tax relief. The value of the shares allocated to any employee in any one year must not exceed £1,250 or, if greater, 10% of the employee's salary under PAYE (excluding benefits in kind) up to a maximum of £5,000 p.a.. If the conditions are met then the payments to the trustees are exempt from corporation tax and the value of the shares allocated to employees are exempt from income tax. Clearly this would be a very tax efficient way for members to build up a capital stake in their business which has two advantages over building up members' reserve accounts. First, the member becomes entitled to the shares as soon as they are allocated whereas golden handshakes have to be voluntary or as a result of the employer's breach of the contract of employment if they are to qualify for tax relief. Secondly, the profits given to the trustees with which to buy shares are immediately exempt from corporation tax whereas profits put to members' reserve accounts have to be found after tax is paid and do not reduce the tax bill until the year in which they are paid out.

Until the 1986 Finance Act worker co-operatives registered under the I & PS Acts could not qualify because one of the conditions was that the shares in the scheme must not be redeemable. The 1986 Act made two changes in favour of worker-controlled businesses, one of which was to permit redeemable shares to qualify in the case of a workers' co-operative.[2] A workers' co-operative is defined in S.24 which provides that it must be a co-operative society registered under the I & PS Acts and that the rules include provisions which secure:

2. Finance Act 1986 S.24(2) amending the Finance Act 1978 9th Schedule Para.7(b).

Income and Corporation Tax

(a) that the only persons who may be members of it are those who are employed by, or by a subsidiary of, the society and those who are the trustees of its profit sharing scheme; and

(b) that, subject to any provision about qualifications for membership which is from time to time made by the members of the society by reference to age, length of service or other factors of any description, all such persons may be members of the society.

S.24 also provides that a workers' co-operative which is seeking approval of its profit sharing scheme shall not cease to be a bona fide co-operative because its rules make provision that the trustees of the scheme may be members, that they may be denied voting rights and that the rules may make such provisions which appear to the Registrar to be reasonably necessary for the purpose of securing approval to the profit sharing scheme.

It is normal for trustees or other joint members to nominate one of their number to be registered as the member and that member then holds the shares as trustee for the joint members.[3] It follows that the joint members count as one member and so profit sharing schemes qualifying for tax relief will not be available for societies with less than six employee members. In order to qualify as soon as there are six employee members we have provided that the committee may require the redemption of the shares of founder members thus clearing the way for an employee only membership. Another consequence of the trustees counting as one member only is that the shareholding remaining in the trustees' hands must never exceed the maximum holding permitted which is currently £10,000. This would not apply if co-operative societies were the only trustees of the scheme, as co-operative societies are exempt from this limitation.[4] These restrictions on membership preclude a co-operative which wants to qualify from having corporate members unless they are trustees of the scheme. However, as a small co-operative may rely on a corporate member which is supplying capital we have left in our model the option to have up to three corporate members. In the early days of a small co-operative the possibility of a profit sharing scheme may seem very remote and later on the rules can always be changed.

The other change in favour of worker-controlled businesses relates to those registered as companies under the Companies Acts. Prior to the 1986 Act the requirements concerning the shares were that they must not be redeemable, that they are ordinary, not preference, shares, fully paid up, not subject to any

---

3. *The Law of Co-operatives* by Ian Snaith (Waterlow Publishers Ltd.) 1984, p.48.
4. I & PS Act 1965 S.6.

restrictions which do not attach to all other shares of the same class and, if the company has more than one class of ordinary shares, then the majority of issued shares of that class must be held by persons other than directors or employees who got their shares by virtue of their office or employment or trustees on their behalf. The 1986 Act has modified the rule concerning restrictions to allow a restriction in the articles requiring shares held by directors and employees to be disposed of on ceasing to be a director or employee so long as the conditions laid down in the Act are met. Also the Act has introduced the concept of employee-control shares which is relevant if there is more than one class of ordinary shares. In that case if the shares are employee-control shares then they are exempt from the requirement that the majority of the issued shares of that class must be held by persons other than directors or employees who got their shares by virtue of their office or employment or trustees on their behalf. In S.23 it is stated that shares are employee-control shares for these purposes if:

(a) the persons holding the shares are, by virtue of their holding, together able to control the company; and
(b) those persons are or have been employees or directors of the company or of another company which is under the control of the company.

Employee shares in our model articles appear to come within these provisions. Under the Finance Act 1978 schedule 9, para.5 the shares in the scheme must form part of the ordinary share capital of the company as defined in S.526(5) of the Taxes Act 1970. This section excludes shares with no right to share in the profits of the company other than a fixed dividend. In our articles the employee members may vote themselves a bonus in addition to the dividend, which may not exceed the prescribed rate, and the employee shares have all the voting rights so must qualify as ordinary shares. By virtue of their voting rights and the fact that they are limited to employees, or trustees of an employee trust, they must qualify as "employee-control shares" within the Act. So, whether or not there are non-voting investor ordinary shares as well as employee shares the employee shares will be available for an approved profit sharing scheme. Alternatively, it might be possible to use investors' shares if a special class of non-voting equity share had been negotiated along the lines discussed in Chapter 2 and if the negotiations included arrangements for selling some of the shares to the trustees of the scheme from time to time and then buying them back.

In the case of companies which have been given, or sold at an undervalue, to the work-force through the medium of an employee trust there is no need for more than one class of ordinary shares and, therefore, no requirement prohibiting the employees holding a majority of the shares. As the company is already in the conventional form there should be no particular problem over setting up a scheme and, if desired, creating a class of employee-control shares.[5] But the problem with any approved profit sharing scheme remains that the employee members will probably want their money out on retirement so some arrangements will need to be made for the purchase of the shares at some time after the release date, perhaps by the trustees. Possible arrangements for this type of company are being explored by JOL. There is a further restriction which could affect a small company and that is that in the case of close companies an employee may not participate in the scheme if the employee and his or her relatives together hold a 25% interest in the company.

Close Companies

Close companies are defined in Part III of the Taxes Act 1970 as including companies under the control of five or fewer participators or of participators who are directors, even if more than five director participators. Societies registered under the I and P S Acts are expressly excluded. Control, under s. 302, includes not only voting control but also the right, or the right to acquire, the greater part of the issued share capital, or the greater part of the income if it was all distributed, or such redeemable share capital as would give on redemption an entitlement to the greater part of the assets available on winding up for distribution amongst members, or the right, in the event of a winding up, to the greater part of the assets available to members.

As most employees of worker-controlled firms are likely to be members it is only small firms which are registered as companies which are likely to be classified as close companies. Although professional advisors may not be too familiar with arrangements for securing worker control they will be very familiar with the concept of close companies and the occasions when this may have a bearing on taxation.

Relief for Interest on Money Borrowed

The right to deduct interest paid out on borrowed money in assessing the individual's liability to income tax depends on what the borrowed money was used for. Schedule I to the Finance Act

---

5. These remarks apply equally where the shares in a conventional company are held by trustees as bare trustees for a democratically elected council of employees as described on p.72.

1974 gives relief if the money is used to acquire ordinary shares of a close company or for a loan to it for the purposes of its business. Although the relief may be available in other circumstances, the individual will usually seek to obtain the relief by establishing the following:

(a) the company is a trading company; and
(b) he or she has not recovered any capital from the company since the proceeds of the loan were applied; and either
(c) he or she has a material interest in the company, i.e., more than 5% of the ordinary share capital; or
(d) he or she holds some of the ordinary share capital and has between the time of the loan and the payment of the interest worked for the greater part of his or her time in the actual management or conduct of the company.

An alternative limb of relief was established with effect from the 10th March 1987: an individual may deduct interest on a loan, which otherwise satisfies the requirements of the Finance Act 1972 S.725, if it was used to acquire a share or shares in a co-operative or in making a loan to such a body which is used wholly and exclusively for its business provided that:

(a) when the interest is paid the body remains a co-operative; and
(b) he or she has worked for the greater part of his or her time as an employee for that body or a subsidiary; and
(c) he or she has not recovered any capital from that body.

For the purposes of the 1981 Act "co-operative" means a common ownership enterprise or a co-operative enterprise as defined in s. 2 of the Industrial Common Ownership Act 1976. To qualify as a common ownership a certificate must be obtained from the Registrar of Friendly Societies that he is satisfied that the company or society complies with a fairly detailed list of requirements which follow closely ICOM's model constitutions, one of them being that members have equal voting rights at meetings. On account of this, ICOM recommend that in cases where the Registrar's certificate may be required there should be no provision for a casting vote which the Registrar might consider contravenes this rule. To qualify as a co-operative a certificate must be obtained from the Secretary of State that he is satisfied that having regard to the provisions in its constitution concerning the application of its income for the benefit of its members and all other relevant provisions it is, in substance, a co-operative association. There is also a requirement in both cases that the body is controlled by a majority of the people working for it. We have included the normal provision for a casting vote in our model constitution as there is no reference in the Act to equal voting in the case of co-operatives, as there is in the case of common ownership, and so no apparent reason for the Secretary of State to take exception to it and it can be very useful. A "co-operative" can be a company just as well as a society.

With effect from April 6th 1983 income tax relief was given to cover interest paid by an individual on money borrowed to acquire any part of the ordinary share capital of an employee-controlled company by a full-time employee or the employee's spouse provided that the company is an unquoted trading company which is resident in the United Kingdom for tax purposes. After the amendments contained in the Finance Act 1984 a company is employee-controlled if at least 50% of the issued ordinary share capital and of the voting power is owned by full-time employees or their spouses. In making this calculation any holding in excess of 10% of the issued share capital held by an individual employee, or the employee and his or her spouse if only one is employed, is treated as though held by a non-employee. The acquisition of the shares must be made before, or not later than one year after, the company first became employee-controlled. This exemption would cover the purchase of a conventional company to be changed to our memorandum and articles within one year when it should qualify under the provisions referred to in the previous paragraph. It is also relevant to management or worker buy-outs where the conventional company structure is retained.

The Business Expansion Scheme

Unlike the relief for interest on money borrowed to put in to a business this relief is for investors who are not connected with the company and being connected includes employees, partners and paid directors. The relief is a deduction for income tax purposes of the amount subscribed for new ordinary shares in an unquoted trading company. The investment in any one year must be at least £500 and not more than £40,000 and to get the full relief the shares must not be sold for a period of five years. Naturally, there are many investors looking for this relief so a worker-controlled company which is prepared to issue a non-voting ordinary share of the type already discussed may well wish to make the shares qualify for the scheme.

There are detailed requirements which are contained in Schedule 5 to the Finance Act 1983, as amended by the following three Finance Acts, which enlarged the business start up scheme introduced by the Finance Act 1981. Paragraph 2(2) limits eligible shares to new ordinary shares which, for five years from the date of issue, carry no present or future preferential right to dividends or assets on winding up and no present or future preferential right to be redeemed. As the Cumulative Convertible Participating Preferred Ordinary Shares evolved by ICFC have a preferential right to dividends they would have to be modified in order to become eligible. This would mean allowing the employee members' special class of voting shares to participate equally in dividends and on winding up. This need not be a major problem since participation is by shareholding and the investing institution could insist on a condition that the employee's shareholding is kept within an agreed limit.

Introduction to the Model Rules and Memorandum and Articles of Association of a Worker Controlled Co-operative

The models provided in this book are designed to serve two purposes. They may either be used in their present forms, with minor amendments to suit the particular cirumstances of each co-operative, or they may be used as guides in the production of rules or articles to suit a particular purpose.

The model rules for an Industrial and Provident Society are considerably more complicated and lengthy than most model rules available. This is deliberate. Whereas a company registered under the Companies Act is provided with a ready made set of rules in the form of Table A, which need only be modified to suit any particular purpose, no such guide exists in the case of an Industrial and Provident Society.

If a Society is to be fully "competitive" with companies when it comes to raising venture capital, or dealing with banks and industry, it would seem prudent to ensure that the rules of the Society are every bit as certain as the rules by which a company is run.

The model rules provided therefore sacrifice brevity and (somewhat unfortunately) simplicity, for the sake of certainty. They also show what provisions may be made if desired, and these provisions can always be transplanted into a shorter set of rules.

The model articles of association are based, as is usual in a private company, on Table A to the Companies Act 1985. This shows that the existing structure of a company can with relative ease be adapted to suit the purposes of a worker controlled enterprise. The only aspect which has not been provided for is the basis on which Investor shares will be issued, but this will depend upon the individual financier and is discussed in the main text.

It must be emphasised that the model rules and the model articles are no more than examples. It is not possible to anticipate every need, although an attempt has been made in the footnotes to provide some guidance. Each co-operative will have its own peculiar circumstances, because of its size, location, type of business, and many other factors. In the case of the rules, references are made to provisions for which statute requires provision to be made. If amending the model, the IPSA 1965 should be studied carefully.

Before adopting any constitution the participants in the co-operative venture should examine very carefully by what rules they are to be governed. At the start of a new venture it is easy to be blinded by optimism and assume that a general consensus will always prevail. It will not. Differences will always arise and must be resolved. Where there is a clear and mandatory method of resolving those differences that resolution will be quick and relatively painless. More than any other structure a workers co-operative will succeed or fail by its ability to manage itself efficiently.

MODEL FORMS OR PRECEDENTS

Worker Controlled Co-Operative Society

RULES OF
LIMITED

registered under the Industrial and Provident Societies Acts 1965-1978 ("the Act")

1. NAME

The name of the Society shall be .... LIMITED[1] ("the Society")

2. OBJECTS[2]

The objects of the Society shall be to carry on as a bona fide co-operative society the business of
[to take over and run as a bona fide co-operative society the business of .... Ltd.] and to carry on any other related business which the Society in General Meeting shall decide to carry on and which is for the benefit of the Society as a whole.

3. POWERS[3]

The Society shall have power to do all things necessary or expedient for the fulfilment of its objects and shall in particular have the power:

(a) to make gifts for social or charitable purposes

(b) to make gifts in support of the co-operative or common ownership movements or to ex-employees of the Society or their dependants in cases of hardship

---

1. S.1(1)(b), Sch.1 para.1. The last word in the name of the Society must be "Limited" unless the registrar is satisfied that the objects are wholly charitable or benevolent. S.5(5).
2. S.1(1)(b), Sch.1 para.2.
3. If it is desired to enable the Society to make political donations this power must be expressly inserted into Rule 3.

(c) to pay pensions to or provide pension benefits for employees or ex-employees or their spouses or dependants save that no member shall receive any of the Society's property save by purchase at full market price or as otherwise provided in these Rules.

4. REGISTERED OFFICE[4]

The registered office of the Society shall be ....

5. MEMBERSHIP

(a) the members of the Society shall be:

   (i) The persons who sign the application for registration under the Act ("founder members") and:
   (ii) The persons whose names are entered in the register of members

(b) Membership of the Society shall be open only to:[5]

   (i) Employees of the Society or of any subsidiary of the Society ("employee members")
   (ii) Societies, Companies and local authorities (being bodies corporate) or nominees of unicorporated associations ("non-employee members")

(c) The Society in General Meeting (the "General Meeting") may make rules from time to time determining the necessary

---

4. S.1(1)(b), Sch.1 para.3. Note that the Act makes provision for certain statutory documents to be available at the registered office and this is the address to which all statutory notices from members may be sent.
5. If the Society is to benefit from the provisions of the Finance Act 1978 relating to approved profit sharing schemes (see text p.74) the amendments set out below must be made in order to qualify under Section 24 of the Finance Act 1986. This does not allow for institutional investors to be members. Replace existing rule 5(b)(ii) with:
"Trustees of a profit sharing scheme for the purpose of securing (and maintaining) approval of such scheme in accordance with Part I of Schedule 9 to the Finance Act 1978 or any statutory modification or re-enactment thereof ('non-employee members')".
Delete sub-rule (g).
Rules 6, 16, 17, 20 and 39 will also require amendments as indicated in notes to those rules.

qualifications required for an employee to become a member. Such qualifications may include requirements for minimum length of service with the Society, minimum hours worked per week, requirements for the purchase of certain quantities of shares in the Society or the maintenance of a loan or reserve account with the Society [or such other conditions as the Society thinks fit]. Such rules shall not require that an employee be employed for a period exceeding [six] months, nor work more than [twenty] hours per week, nor contribute a sum exceeding that employee's gross salary by way of share purchase, loan or reserve account. No employee shall be excluded from membership on grounds of race, religion or sex.[6]

(d) A body corporate which is a member may by resolution of its governing body appoint and revoke the appointment of any person to represent it at any general meeting of the Society. Such person shall be entitled, on behalf of the body corporate, to exercise all the rights and powers of the body corporate as if the body corporate were an individual member. A copy of the resolution appointing such person, signed by two members of the governing body of the body corporate and in the case of a local authority by the Clerk of the Council shall be sent to the Secretary of the Society.

(e) A member who is the nominee of an unincorporated body shall have entered against his name in the register of members the name of that body.

(f) No person below the age of 18[7] shall be a member of the Society.

(g) The number of non-employee members shall not exceed three.[8]

---

6. The notes of guidance for the registration of societies issued by the Registry of Friendly Societies ("the notes of guidance") indicate that there should be no artificial restriction of membership with the object of increasing the value of proprietary rights and interests. Although the making of qualifying rules is left to the General Meeting, the principle is sound. The rules should therefore attempt to balance ease of entry with the requirements of stability and equal contribution.
7. This limit may be lowered to 16 years, IPSA 1965, S.20.
8. This would prevent non-employee members from forming a majority with a minimum membership of seven.

6. APPLICATION FOR MEMBERSHIP[9]

(a) Any person qualifying for membership as an employee member and wishing to apply shall send [the sum of £1] such sum as shall be required in accordance with rule 5(c) above being the sum of £1] for each share applied for together with an application for membership to the Secretary at the Registered Office of the Society. The Committee shall at its next meeting consider the application and shall accept the application subject only to the provisions of Rule 5 above. If the application is refused the applicant's money shall be returned as soon as possible thereafter. If successful the applicant shall be sent a copy of the Rules and issued with one share for each £1 paid. The Secretary shall make an appropriate entry in the register of members. No share certificate need be issued to any member.

(b)[10] Any society or corporation investing funds in the Society under the provisions of the Act shall be admitted to membership if such admission is first approved by The General Meeting on the terms and conditions of these Rules together with such additional terms and conditions as may be agreed between that person and the Society.

7. TERMINATION OF MEMBERSHIP

(a) A person shall cease to be a member on:

(i) In the case of an employee member ceasing to be employed by the Society;
(ii) ceasing to fulfil any relevant qualification for membership specified in or made pursuant to Rule 5;
(iii) the transfer of all that member's shares to another person or such number of shares as reduces that member's shareholding below the minimum required by Rule 8;
(iv) resigning membership by giving 28 days notice in writing to the Secretary;

But (i) and (iv) above shall not operate without the prior approval

---

9. S.1(1)(b) Sch.1 para4.
 Any employee of the Society or of a subsidiary of the Society who qualifies for membership must be admitted. This is in any case required by paragraph 18 in Schedule 9 to the Finance Act 1978 if the Society is to qualify under that Act.
10. If the rules are to qualify under the F.A. 1986 S.24 (see note to rule 5(b)), sub-rule 6(b) should be deleted and sub-rule 6(1) becomes Rules 6.

of the General Meeting if to do so were to reduce the number of members below seven.

(b) On cessation of membership the provisions of Rule 10 shall apply with regard to the repayment of share capital.

8. SHARES

(a) The share capital of the Society shall consist of shares of the nominal value of £1 each.

(b) Each member shall hold a minimum of [1]share[s], or such other number as is determined by the Society in General Meeting from time to time, and a maximum of 10,000[11] shares or such other maximum number as is permitted by law.

(c) Interest on shares may be paid at such a rate not exceeding 2% above the base lending rate of the [Co-Operative Bank PLC] or 6% per annum whichever is the higher as shall be determined from time to time by the Society in general meeting.[12] The rate so determined shall not exceed that recommended by the Committee which shall be such rate as is necessary for the Society to raise and maintain its capital. If no such rate is determined in respect of any financial year of the Society, the rate of interest payable on shares shall be nil.

(d) Shares in the Society shall not be withdrawable.[13]

(e) On the death of a member that member's shares shall be cancelled, and shall be treated as having been redeemed in accordance with Rule 10(c).[14]

11. Industrial and Provident Societies (Increase in Shareholding Limit) Order 1981.
12. The notes of guidance suggest that the rate of return on shares should be limited. This is consistent with achieving a return related to participation, not capital. It is understood that the rates inserted are the highest that will be accepted by the Registrar at the present time.
13. S.1(1)(b) para.9.
14. S.1(1)(b) para.9.
    It may be that shares are issued to investors which it is desired to make not freely transferable. This rule should then be altered accordingly. However, as there may be a limit on the number of non-employee members (three in the Model Rules) and such members cannot be in a majority at meetings it may be advantageous to make such shares as attractive as possible. If the Rules are to qualify under the F.A. 1986 S.24 (see note to rule 5(b)) then the rules must prohibit the holding of shares by non-employee investors.

9. TRANSFER OF SHARES

(a) Shares shall be transferable provided that upon transfer the transferee holds the necessary qualifications for membership and does not by virtue of the transfer exceed the permitted maximum shareholding or thereby cause the number of members to fall below seven.

(b) A person wishing to transfer shares shall give notice in writing to the Secretary giving details of the shares to be transferred. The notice shall be signed by the transferor and the transferee, to the effect that the transferee, if not otherwise a member, thereby applies for membership and agrees to be bound by these Rules and the conditions attached to the shares.

(c) The notice of transfer shall be placed before the Committee at the next Committee meeting and the Committee shall accept the transfer if in accordance with these Rules. The appropriate entries shall be made in the register of members.

10. REDEMPTION OF SHARES

(a) The Society shall have the power to redeem its shares.

(b) The Committee shall require the redemption of a member's shares (other than a non-employee member's shares) when that member ceases to be employed by the Society or any of its subsidiaries.

(c) The Committee may require the redemption of a member's shares where:
- (i) the member ceases to hold the necessary qualifications imposed by Rule 5;
- (ii) The member holds shares in excess of the minimum required by Rule 8(b) and the Committee desires to redeem such number of shares as does not reduce the member's shareholding below such minimum in accordance with such policy as the Society in General Meeting may from time to time determine with regard to desired levels of member's shareholdings;
- (iii) the member has resigned in accordance with Rule 7(a) (iv);
- (iv) the member is a member who qualifies only by virtue of being a founder member under Rule 5(a)(i) or is a non-employee member under Rule 5(b)(ii);

(d) The Society shall redeem shares by giving 28 days notice in writing of redemption to a member. Where redemption is in accordance with (b) or (c)(iii) no such notice shall be necessary.

(e) Upon redemption a share shall be cancelled and the appropriate entry made in the register of members.

(f) Redemption of any share in accordance with this rule shall be at par save that if the Committee is of the opinion that the net asset value of the Society attributable to that share is less than par the Committee may instruct the Society's auditors (acting as experts not as arbitrators) to value the share on a net asset basis. The auditor's valuation shall be conclusive and shall, if less than par but not otherwise, be the redemption price of the share.

11. PAYMENT FOR REDEEMED SHARES

On the redemption of any share in accordance with Rule 10 the Committee may require that some or all of the sum due on the shares so redeemed be carried to that member's loan account and repaid in accordance with the provisions of Rule 37. Such sums as are not carried to that member's loan account shall be paid in cash within 28 days of redemption or in such other manner as shall be agreed between that member and the Committee. Sums due on redemption of a share shall include all dividend or interest which has accrued up to the date of redemption.

12. BORROWING POWERS

(a) The Society shall have the power to borrow money for its purposes and shall have the power to give security over its property. The total amount borrowed by the society shall not exceed [£1,000,000] or such other sum as shall be determined from time to time by the Society in General Meeting.[15]

(b) The rate of interest on money borrowed, except on money borrowed by way of bank overdraft or loan or on mortgage from a building society or local authority or borrowed from any financial institution, shall not exceed 6% per annum of 2% above the [Co-operative Bank PLC] base lending rate, whichever is the higher.

(c) The Society shall not take deposits.

15. S.1(1)(b) para.8

13. INVESTMENT POWERS

The funds of the Society may with the authority of the Committee be invested in any of the following ways:[16]

(a) In any way authorised by Section 31 of the Act namely;

   (i) in any security being a security in which trustees are for the time being authorised by law to invest;
   (ii) in or upon any mortgage, bond, debenture, debenture stock, corporation stock, annuity, rentcharge, rent or other security (not being securities payable to bearer) authorised by or under any Act of any local authority within the meaning of the Local Loans Act 1875;
   (iii) in the shares or on the security of any other registered society, of any society registered under the Building Societies Acts, or of any company registered under the Companies Acts or incorporated by Act of Parliament or by charter, being a company with limited liability.

(b) In such other manner as is authorised from time to time by the Society in General Meeting.

(c) The Committee may appoint one or more of its members to represent the Society and vote on its behalf at any meetings of any body at which the Society is so entitled.

(d) [In the shares of   Limited].[17]

14. ANNUAL GENERAL MEETINGS[18]

(a) The Society shall hold its first annual general meeting ("AGM") within 18 months of the date of registration of the Society, at such time and place as the Committee shall decide. Each subsequent AGM shall be held not less than six months after the close of the financial year of the Society.

(b) The business of the AGM shall include:

---

16. S.1(1)(b) para.14.
17. It may be that the Society is formed with the express intention of acquiring an existing company or society. That should be reflected in the objects, but this sub-rule should also be inserted.
18. S1(1)(b) para.5

(i) the election of the Committee;
(ii) the consideration of the Society's accounts and balance sheet for the last financial year and the reports of the Committee and the auditor thereon;
(iii) the appointment of an auditor for the current financial year;
(iv) the transaction of such other business as the Committee shall decide and such business as shall have been notified to the Committee by any members at least [   ] days prior to the AGM.

15. EXTRAORDINARY GENERAL MEETINGS

The Committee may at any time convene an extraordinary general meeting ("EGM") and shall do so on a written requisition signed by not less than one tenth of the members or [10] members which ever is the less ("the requisitionists")[19] stating the purpose for which the meeting is to be convened. If within 14 days of delivery of such requisition to the registered office no valid notices convening a meeting for the stated purpose have been sent out to members, the requisitionists may themselves convene a meeting for the stated purpose in the manner provided by Rule 16. The requisitionists shall be entitled to reimbursement from the Society of all sums reasonably spent in convening the meeting.

16. NOTICE[20]

(a) A general meeting shall be convened by giving all members 14 clear days notice in writing. The notice shall specify the day, hour and place of the meeting, whether an AGM or EGM and shall state the general nature of the business to be conducted at the meeting.

(b) Alternatively,[21] if authorised generally by a general meeting

---

19. For alternative provision see Article of Association No.15.
20. If the Rules are to qualify under the F.A. 1986 S.24 (see note to rule 5(b)) add a new sub-rule (e):
    (e) A non-employee member shall be entitled to receive notices of, attend, and speak at any meeting of the Society but shall not (unless also a member in their own right) count towards any quorum or vote.
21. In a Society where every member works in the same location it may be appropriate to give notice 'informally' by prominently displaying notices for a meeting. Nevertheless, if very contentious business is likely to be transacted, individual written notices would be sensible.

convened in accordance with sub-rule (a), a general meeting may be convened by the posting of a notice to that effect 14 days in advance of the meeting in such prominent place or places so as the notice is likely to come to the attention of all the members. The notice shall specify the day, hour and place of the meeting, whether an AGM or EGM and shall state the general nature of the business to be conducted at the meeting.

(c) The accidental omission to give any member notice of a general meeting or the non-receipt of a notice by any member shall not invalidate the proceedings at the meeting.

(d) A general meeting shall be deemed to have been properly convened if all the members of the Society are present in person or by proxy and agree that the meeting shall be deemed to have been properly convened.

17. QUORUM

(a) No business shall be transacted at any general meeting unless a quorum of members is present at the time the meeting proceeds to business. Except as provided in sub-rule (b) [5][22] members present in person shall be a quorum [and except as provided in sub-rule (b) no meeting shall be quorate where there is present a majority of non-employee members].[23]

(b) If within half an hour of the time appointed for the meeting a quorum is not present the meeting, if convened upon the requisition of members, shall be dissolved. In any other case the meeting shall stand adjourned for seven days to the same time and place, or to such other day, time and place as shall be decided upon by the Committee. If adjoured to a time and place decided by the Committee, seven clear days notice of the adjourned meeting shall be given to all members. If at the adjourned meeting a quorum is not present then those members present shall be a quorum.

22. To ensure that decisions are taken by the membership as a whole it is desirable that the quorum be higher than in an ordinary company. Thus a proportionate figure such as 'three quarters of the employee members' might be used. The rule could provide for a quorum to consist of every member, or every employee member, but this would stifle decision making if even one person were unable or unwilling to attend.
23. If the rules are to qualify under the F.A. 1986 S.24 (see note to rule 5(b)) delete the words in square brackets and replace with the words: "Non-employee members shall not count towards a quorum".

18. CONDUCT OF THE MEETING

The Chairperson of the Committee shall preside over the general meeting. If within 15 minutes of the time appointed for the meeting no such person is present, the members present shall elect from their number a person to chair the meeting. Prior to such election the Secretary, if present, shall have the conduct of the meeting. If the meeting is unable to agree upon a Chairperson the member present whose name appears first in the register of members shall act as Chairperson for that meeting.

19. ADJOURNMENTS

The Chairperson of a meeting may with the consent of the meeting, and shall if so directed by the meeting, adjourn the meeting from time to time and place to place. Only business left unfinished from the original meeting shall be conducted at the adjourned meeting. Unless the time and place of the adjourned meeting are announced to the original meeting, seven clear days notice of the adjourned meeting shall be given to all members.

20. VOTING

(a) At any general meeting a resolution put to the vote shall, subject to any requirement in the Act or these Rules, be decided by simple majority of those members present at the meeting. A resolution shall be decided on a show of hands unless before or on the declaration of the result a poll is demanded by the Chairperson or by not less than [2] members present in person or by proxy. The demand for a poll may be withdrawn but only before the poll is taken and with the consent of the Chairperson. A demand so withdrawn shall not be taken to have invalidated the result of a show of hands so declared before the demand was made.

(b) Unless a poll is demanded a declaration by the Chairperson that a resolution has on a show of hands been carried, or carried unanimously, or by a particular majority, or lost shall be conclusive evidence of the number or proportion of votes recorded for or against a resolution. If a poll is demanded before the declaration of the result of a show of hands and the demand is duly withdrawn, the meeting shall continue as if the demand had not been made.

(c) A poll demanded on the election of a Chairperson or on a question of adjournment shall be taken at once. A poll demanded on any other question shall be taken at such time as the Chairperson of the meeting directs being not more than thirty days after the poll is demanded. Any other business may be proceeded with pending the taking of the poll. The result of the poll shall be deemed to be the resolution of the meeting at which the poll was demanded.

(d) On a show of hands every member present in person shall have one vote and on a poll every member present in person or by proxy shall have one vote. In the case of an equality of votes, whether on a show of hands or on a poll, the chairperson of the meeting at which the show of hands takes place or at which the poll was demanded shall have a second or casting vote.[24]

(e) No objection shall be raised to the qualification of any person to vote except at the meeting or adjourned meeting at which that vote is tendered. Any objection made in due time shall be referred to the Chairperson of the meeting whose decision shall be final and conclusive. Any vote not disallowed shall be valid for all purposes.

(f) A resolution in writing signed by all the members (and in the case of non-employee members signed by their duly authorised representative) for the time being entitled to receive notice of and to attend and vote at general meetings shall be as valid and effective as if that resolution had been passed at a general meeting duly convened and held. Several documents in the same or similar form each signed by one or more members may

---

24. This rule gives the Chairperson a casting vote. ICOM omit this power because the Industrial Common Ownership Act 1976 specifies that members have equal voting rights. There is no such requirement for a co-operative society and it may be wished to substitute commercial certainty for possible deadlock. If the members are able, as is desirable, to proceed by way of consensus rather than by taking votes, this provision is not in any event necessary. It may be thought desirable to make a provision for the chair to 'rotate' amongst members at meetings.
    If the Rules are to qualify under the F.A. 1986 S.24 (see note to rule 5(b)), delete sub-rule (d) and substitute the following sub-rule:
    (d) On a show of hands every member other than a non-employee member present in person shall have one vote and on a poll every member other than a non-employee member present in person or by proxy shall have one vote. A non-employee member shall not have the right to vote at any meeting of the Society. In the case of an equality of votes, whether on a show of hands or on a poll, the Chairperson of the meeting at which the show of hands takes place or at which the poll was demanded shall have a second or casting vote.

constitute a written resolution. The provisions of this sub-rule shall not apply to an AGM.

21. PROXIES

Any member or duly appointed representative of a non-employee member may appoint a proxy to attend a meeting and speak and vote on that member's behalf. A proxy need not be a member. Every such appointment shall be in writing signed by the member or representative making it or under that person's authority. A form of proxy shall be valid for any business conducted at a meeting provided a copy thereof was delivered to the registered office at least 24 hours prior to the meeting. A form of proxy shall be in writing, signed by the appointor and shall be in any form which is usual or which the Committee may allow. The Committee shall allow any form which indicates unambiguously the wish of a member to appoint a particular person or persons as proxy.

22. POWERS AND FUNCTION OF THE COMMITTEE

(a) The management of the Society shall be conducted by the Committee which shall act for and in the name of the Society. The Committee shall exercise all the powers of the Society which are not, by statute or by these Rules or by resolution of the General Meeting, conferred solely upon the Society in general meeting.

(b) The Committee may delegate any of its powers to any sub-committee comprised of Committee members. Any sub-committee so formed shall proceed under the instructions of the Committee which shall at all times retain a concurrent and superior jurisdiction over all matters delegated. A sub-committee shall conduct itself in accordance with these rules, but the minimum number of members on a sub-committee shall be [2].

23. COMPOSITION OF THE COMMITTEE[25]

(a) The Committee shall comprise not less than [7] and not more

---

25. S1(1)(b) para.6
    In a small society it is desirable that every member also be a member of the Committee. An additional sub-rule could be added as (a) requiring a re-lettering of the present sub-rules and providing that:

than [15] persons. Committee members need not be members of the Society but not less than half of the Committee shall be members of the Society.

(b) Until the end of the first general meeting of the Society the persons who signed the application for registration of the Society shall comprise the Committee.

(c) From the end of the first general meeting of the Society the Committee shall comprise those persons elected at that meeting in accordance with Rule 25. If no such election takes place the existing Committee members shall be deemed duly elected at that meeting.

(d) The Committee may from time to time and subject to sub-rule (a) hereof co-opt any suitable person to serve on the Committee, and may remove such persons. A co-opted Committee member may speak and vote at meetings of the Committee.

24. CASUAL VACANCIES

If a vacancy caused be the retirement or removal of a Committee member other than a co-opted member is not filled otherwise in accordance with these Rules, the Committee may appoint a person to fill the vacancy. The person so appointed shall for all purposes be treated as a duly elected Committee member, and shall retire accordingly at the next AGM. A vacancy shall be deemed to exist if the Committee is comprised of either less than the minimum number required by Rule 23(a) or less than the number of Committee Members elected at the last AGM.[26]

25. APPONTMENT OF COMMITTEE[27]

    (a) "If and for so long as the number of employee members of the Society does not exceed 15 every employee member who signs a declaration of willingness to act shall be a member of the Committee. Until such time Rules 23(b) to 26 and Rule 27(i), (vi) and (vii) shall not apply to the Society".
    Under Rule 22 the Committee may delegate powers to sub-committees, thus the task of administration can be divided up amongst smaller groups.
26.   The quorum requirement in Rule 32 ensures that the non-members cannot be an effective majority.
27.   S.1(1)(b) para. 6.
    In a large society it may be desirable to ensure that particular groups of employees who are in a minority are able to be represented on the Committee. If this cannot be achieved by agreement, provision may be made

(a) At the end of each AGM all the members of the Committee shall retire. A member of the Committee so retiring, other than a member co-opted under Rule 23(d), shall be taken to be standing for re-election to the Committee unless that person declares a wish not to be re-elected

(b) Any member wishing to stand for election to the Committee shall, not less than seven days before the date appointed for the meeting at which that person intends to seek appointment, deliver to the registered office of the Society a notice to that effect

(c) Any non member of the Society may stand for election to the Committee if nominated by a member. The nomination shall be in writing, signed by the member, and contain a signed statement by the person nominated of willingness to act. The nomination shall be delivered to the registered office not less than seven days before the date appointed for the meeting. A non-member of the Society may however stand for re-election under sub-rule (a) without further nomination.

(d) The General Meeting shall decide, within the limits imposed by Rule 23(a), on the number of vacancies on the Committee. The General Meeting shall then attempt to fill those vacancies by electing a Committee from the persons standing for election or for re-election. On the election of a Committee each member of the Society shall have one vote for each vacancy to be filled, but shall cast no more than one vote for each candidate. In the event that the General Meeting is unable to fill all the vacancies, or is unwilling to do so from the candidates available, the General Meeting may appoint to the Committee any member or members who express at the meeting a willingness to act on the Committee notwithstanding that no notice was given by that member in accordance with sub-rule (b).

(e) At the end of each AGM the new Committee shall take office. If no elections have taken place for a new Committee the existing Committee shall be deemed to have been re-elected.

> in the rules either by making specific provision or by adopting some form of proportional representation. Thus Rule 23 might read:
> "The General Meeting shall elect the Committee by proportional representation with single transferable vote with quota and eliminative counting in accordance with the rules presented by the Electoral Reform Society who may be requested by the Society to conduct the election. In the event of any dispute over the election of candidates the dispute shall be referred to the arbitration of a single arbitrator appointed by the president for the time being of the Electoral Reform Society whose decision shall be final".
> In this way the Committee may more fairly represent the employees.

(f) The General Meeting shall decide upon the remuneration, if any, of the Committee. The Committee shall have the power to remunerate any ad-hoc Committee member, or person appointed to fill a casual vacancy, at a rate not exceeding the average remuneration for the existing remunerated members (if any) of the Committee. No member of the Committee who is also an employee of the Society shall be remunerated for duties carried out as a member of the Committee (but may receive remuneration as an employee or for other services of value provided to the Society).

26. REMOVAL OF COMMITTEE MEMBERS

(a) The Society may in any general meeting remove any member of the Committee from office. No resolution for the removal of a Committee member shall be valid unless proper notice has been given of that resolution in accordance with Rule 16.

(b) The short-notice provisions of Rule 16(d) shall apply to this Rule, as shall the provisions of Rule 20(f), but a Committee member who has been removed without the opportunity of making reasonable oral or written representations to a general meeting of the Society shall be entitled to requisition a meeting of the Society in accordance with the provisions of Rule 15. In that case the person removed shall be entitled to requisition a meeting on that person's signature alone but may call the meeting only for the purpose of having the removal set aside.[28]

(c) On the removal of a Committee member or at a subsequent meeting called to set aside or ratify that removal the General Meeting may, or if the removal reduces the Committee below the number specified in Rule 23(a) the General Meeting shall, appoint another person to the Committee.

27. DISQUALIFICATION

A person shall cease to be a member of the Committee if that person:

28. It may be that a committee member who is not a member of the Society is removed because of a disagreement with a majority. Such a person should be given an opportunity to explain to the meeting why they should not be removed. This can provide a valuable chance for non-committee members to hear an independent voice which would otherwise not be heard.

(i) is removed from office in accordance with Rule 26;
(ii) is adjudicated bankrupt or makes any composition or scheme of arrangement with their creditors generally;
(iii) becomes a patient within the meaning of Part VII of the Mental Health Act 1983 or its equivalent in any other country or an order is made by a court having jurisdiction (whether in the United Kingdom or elsewhere) in matters concerning mental disorder for his detention or for the appointment of a receiver, curator bonis or other person to exercise powers with respect to that person's property or affairs;
(iv) resigns office by giving notice in writing to the Committee;
(v) being a member of the Society on appointment to the Committee ceases for whatever reason to be a member. (But that person shall subject to Rule 23(a) be eligible for co-option to the Committee in accordance with Rule 23(d));
(vi) is absent from [four] consecutive meetings of the Committee without special leave of absence, such leave to be given by the Committee or by the General Meeting, and the Committee so resolve;
(vii) fails to declare an interest in any contract or dealing in accordance with Rule 28. In such a case the Committee, being of the opinion that such failure has taken place and was not both in respect of a trivial interest and the result of inadvertence shall pass a resolution to that effect. The person shall cease at once to be a Committee Member, but may be reinstated by the General Meeting.

28. INTEREST IN CONTRACTS[29]

(a) Any Committee member who is personally interested, whether directly or indirectly, in any contract or dealing entered into, or proposed to be entered into by the Society, shall declare the interest at every Committee meeting at which that matter arises. Such person shall not vote on any resolution regarding that matter, or if a vote is taken that person's vote shall not be counted. Any resolution passed only by virtue of that person's vote shall be invalid, and an appropriate entry made in the books

---

29. Most small private companies allow directors to deal with the company. This seems inappropriate in a co-operative environment without at least some safeguards. Members who are not Committee members could deal with the Society because the Committee will enter into any contract on behalf of the Society and can exercise independent control over its terms to ensure that the Society is protected. See Article of Association No.25.

of the Society. This Rule shall not invalidate any contract between the Society and any person who entered into that contract without notice of the Committee member's interest.

(b) A Committee member may be interested in any contract or dealing, and vote theron, or may act in competition with the Society, if such activity is approved by resolution of the General Meeting, to which full disclosure of all relevant matters has been made by the interested person.

(c) The Committee may remove a member of the Committee from office if it is of the opinion, and passes a resolution to the effect that that person is unsuited to be a member of the Committee by reason of the nature of their interests declared under this Rule, or by reason of that person's trading in competition with the Society or being involved in any business which is in competition with the Society, or is in any other way competing with the Society. Such person, if reinstated by the General Meeting, shall not again be removed by the Committee by reason of any matter which was before that General Meeting.

29. CHAIRPERSON

The Committee shall at its first meeting, and at every subsequent first meeting following an AGM, elect a Chairperson who shall have conduct of Committee meetings. The Chairperson shall be a member of the Society. The Chairperson shall hold office until the end of the next AGM of the Society unless removed from that office by the Committee, or by the General Meeting, or until ceasing to be a Committee member, or a member of the Society.

30. MEETINGS

(a) The Committee shall meet as often as is required for the proper conduct of the Society's business and in any case at least once a [month]. Any Committee member may, and on the requisition of any Committee member the Secretary shall, convene a Committee meeting.

(b) If the Chairperson is absent from any meeting, that meeting shall elect a Chairperson for the purposes of that meeting only. Prior to the election of a Chairperson the Secretary, if present, shall have the conduct of the meeting. If the meeting cannot agree upon a Chairperson, the person present whose name first appears in the register of members shall act as Chairperson for that meeting.

31. NOTICE

Every Committee Member shall be given reasonable notice of every meeting, and unless the circumstances require that longer or shorter notice be given, seven days notice in writing shall be deemed reasonable.[30] The accidental omission to give notice to, or the non-receipt of notice by, a Committee member shall not invalidate the proceedings of the meeting.

32. QUORUM

The quorum for a meeting of the Committee shall be [three] but at a meeting where less than half the Committee members present are members of the Society no business shall be transacted save that of adjourning the meeting, or convening a general meeting of the Society. If the Committee has fallen below the number required for a quorum the Committee may continue to act for one month but thereafter shall have no power save the power to convene a general meeting for the purpose of appointing new Committee members.

33. VOTING

(a) Any questions arising for decision at a Committee meeting shall be decided by simple majority. In the case of an equality of votes the votes of non-members of the Society shall be discounted to obtain a result. If there still remains an equality of votes the Chairperson shall have a second or casting vote, or shall be entitled to convene a general meeting for the purpose of deciding that question.

(b) A resolution in writing signed by all the Committee members entitled to receive notice of a meeting of the Committee shall be as valid and effective as if it had been passed at a meeting of the Committee duly convened and held.

---

30. Seven days notice in writing is a 'failsafe'. Shorter and oral notice will usually suffice as being reasonable but this will usually depend upon the agenda.

34. SECRETARY AND OTHER OFFICERS[31]

(a) The Committee shall appoint a Secretary whose remuneration, if any, shall be determined by the Committee. The Committee may revoke the appointment but shall in that case appoint another person to the office. The Committee may appoint and revoke the appointment of any other person to such office as the Committee think fit, with such responsibilities and subject to Rule 25(f) at such remuneration as the Committee think fit.

(b) The duties of the Secretary shall be determined by these Rules and by the Committee but the Secretary shall in any case:

    (i) summon and attend meetings of the Society and of the Committee and keep minutes thereof;
    (ii) maintain and keep the register of members, and other registers required to be kept by the Act or by these rules;
    (iii) submit to the Registrar appropriate notices of any changes in these Rules, or of a change in the registered office of the Society, and make all other returns to the Registrar as are required by these rules or by the Act;
    (iv) unless the Committee otherwise direct, keep all the books of account and receive all contributions and other payments due from members and other person to the Society and pay over the amount so received as the Society shall direct;
    (v) give such access to the books or property of the Society which are in the Secretary's possession as shall be required by these Rules, or by the Committe, or by the General Meeting;
    (vi) have charge of the seal of the Society.

(c) The Secretary shall be provided with a copy of these Rules, a copy of the Act, and a copy of the Friendly and Industrial and Provident Societies Act 1968.

(d) Anything which may be done by or to the Secretary and a member of the Committee shall not be done by or to the same person acting in both capacities.

[(e) The Secretary shall be a member of the Society.]

---

31. Certain functions are required by statute to be carried out by the secretary; a secretary must therefore be appointed. It is common for a company's accountant to act as secretary, but such a person would no doubt require payment for that task.

35. MINUTES

The Committee shall ensure that proper minutes of its proceedings are kept and entered in the minute book of the Society. The Chairperson of the meeting shall sign each minute of the previous meeting. Unless the Committee otherwise decides the Secretary shall take the minutes and have charge of the book, which may be inspected by any member of the Society. The Committee shall also ensure that proper minutes of the proceedings of the general meetings of the Society are taken and kept in a like manner. Any member of the Society shall be entitled to inspect the minutes of the general meetings.

36. THE SEAL[32]

The Society shall have a seal which shall be kept by the Secretary. The seal shall be used by authority of the Committee and any instrument to which it is affixed shall be signed by a member of the Committee and countersigned by the Secretary or by another member of the Committee appointed for that purpose by the Committee.

37. MEMBERS' LOAN ACCOUNTS[33]

(a) The Society shall keep an account of all sums received from members or credited as received from members by way of loan. Such loans shall be subject to Rule 12 and shall carry interest at [a rate of ... % or] such rate as may be decided by the General Meeting from time to time. Such rate shall not exceed the maximum interest payable on shares in accordance with Rule 8(c). The terms of members' loans to the Society shall be determined by the General Meeting but in default of such determination as to repayment the loan shall be repayable on notice by the Society, or on demand by a member giving 28 days notice in writing to the Secretary. If no such terms are agreed as to interest, interest shall accrue at the simple rate (if any) prevailing for interest on shares.

---

32. S.1(1)(b) Sch.1, para.13.
33. S.1(1)(b) para.8.
    The Rules as drafted provide both for interest to be paid on loans as well as for repayment 28 days after demand. It would be wise for members to agree on less onerous terms of repayment, as one dissenting member might, when cash flow was tight, be able to wind up the Society. Payment could be by way of monthly or even yearly instalments.

(b) The General Meeting may from time to time make rules or policies requiring that members must or should maintain a minimum balance outstanding on loan to the Society. Such rules may make the contracting of such loan a condition of membership. No employee shall as a condition of membership be required to lend a sum in excess of [£1000] or [one quarter of their annual salary] to the Society, whichever is the higher.

38. MEMBERS' RESERVE ACCOUNTS

(a) The Society may keep accounts called "members' reserve accounts" recording all retained profits credited to members' reserve accounts and sums received from members or credited as received from members by way of contribution to the Society for the credit of that member's reserve account. Such sums shall be the absolute property of the Society.

(b) The Committee shall recommend what proportion of retained profit, including unrealised profit, if any, is available for credit to members' reserve accounts. The provisions of Rule 39(d) shall apply to this rule as if sums to be credited to members' reserve accounts were profits to be distributed.

(c) The Society may pay interest on members' reserve accounts in accordance with Rule 39(b)(iii).

(d) On cessation of membership the Society may take into account the amount standing to the credit of a member's reserve account in deciding what sum, if any, to pay to that member as compensation for loss of office, or as a gratuity. Any sum so paid shall reduce that member's reserve account accordingly.

(e) The General Meeting may make rules requiring that on cessation of membership any sum standing to the credit of a member's reserve account shall be paid to that member or treated as if it were a sum standing to the credit of a member's loan account or as if it were comprised of shares in the Society.[34] In the absence of such rules the Society shall not be obliged to pay any sum in respect of a member's reserve account and the sum standing to the credit of that account shall for all purposes be treated as part of the Society's general capital.

---

34. If such a rule is made then the tax exemption relating to compensation for loss of office or gratuity on retiring may well be lost.

(f) The General Meeting may at any time resolve that the total sum standing to the credit of all members' reserve accounts be carried to the general reserves of the Society.

39. APPLICATION OF PROFITS[35]

(a) The Committee shall recommend what profit if any is available for distribution in any year. Such profit as is not distributed shall be retained in a general reserve for the continuation and development of the Society or in members' reserve accounts under Rule 38.

(b) The profits of the Society not retained shall be applied as follows in such manner and in such proportion as decided upon by the Society in General Meeting. Profit may be used for:

(i) the payment of interest on shares in accordance with Rule 8(c);

(ii) the payment of interest on members' reserve accounts at a rate not exceeding the maximum interest payable on shares under Rule 8(c);

(iii) the payment to members of bonus payments equally or in such other proportion as decided by the General Meeting and which is related to their participation in the Society but not to their shareholding.[36]

(c) Payment shall be by way of:

(i) cash distribution;
(ii) credit to a member's loan account;
(iii) the allocation of bonus shares treated as paid up. No

---

35. S.1(1)(b) para.12.
    If the Rules are to qualify under the F.A. 1986 S.24 (see note to Rule 5(b)) the following additions should be made:
    "(b) (v) the payment to the trustees of an approved profit sharing scheme for the purposes of the scheme;
    (c) (iv) the allocation of bonus shares treated as paid up to the trustees of an approved profit sharing scheme whether or not such trustees are existing members of the Society".
36. The members may prefer to make bonus payments not equally but according to the member's salary or earnings as reflecting the value of their participation.

member shall be allocated such number of bonus shares as would raise that member's shareholding above the permitted maximum in Rule 8(b).

(d) If authorised by the General Meeting to carry out any policy of the Society with regard to members holding particular sums in loan account or with regard to the preferred level of shareholding of each member, the Committee shall have the power to allocate a member's share of distributed profit on an individual basis in such manner as it thinks fit in order to comply with such policies.

(e) In any year any sum standing to the credit of the general reserve and representing profit for that year or undistributed profit from previous years may, if the Committee so recommends and the General Meeting so approves, be applied as profit in any way authorised by this Rule.

40. BOOKS AND RECORDS[37]

(a) The Society shall keep at its registered office a register of members containing particulars of:

   (i) the names and addresses of members;
   (ii) a statement of the number of shares held by each member and of the amount paid or agreed to be considered as paid on the shares of each member;
   (iii) a statement of other property in the society, whether in loans, deposits or otherwise, held by each member;
   (iv) the date at which each person was entered in the register and the date at which any person ceased to be a member;
   (v) the names and addresses of the officers (including the members of the Committee), with the offices held by them respectively and the dates on which they assumed office.

(b) The Secretary shall maintain the details of the register of members and any member or officer of the Society shall notify the Secretary of any change of address.

(c) The Secretary shall ensure that the register of members is maintained in accordance with the Act, and shall if necessary maintain a duplicate register or otherwise construct the register

---

37. S.44.1. Note that by Section 40 of the Act a copy of the latest balance sheet and auditors report is to be displayed in a conspicuous position at the registered office. See Rule 45(c).

of members such that the particulars required by the Act to be available for inspection are readily accessible without the need to disclose the other particulars contained in the register.

41. INSPECTION OF BOOKS[38]

(a) The register of members shall be available for inspection at the registered office between 9 a.m. and 5 p.m. on each weekday or at such other reasonable times as shall be decided by the General Meeting.

(b) A member shall be entitled to inspect the register of members but shall not unless a member of the Committee be entitled to inspect the loan or share account of any other person without that person's written consent or the authority of the General Meeting.

(c) Any person having an interest in the funds of the Society shall be allowed to inspect details of that person's own account and all the particulars contained in the register of members save for those specified in Rule 40(a)(ii) and (iii).

(d) Any member of the Committee or other officer of the Society may inspect any of the Society's books.

(e) Any person entitled to inspect any book or record of the Society shall be entitled to take copies thereof, and if the Society makes provision for such copying (which it shall not be obliged to do) it may charge a reasonable sum therefor.

42. COPIES OF THE RULES[39]

A copy of these Rules and any amendments thereto shall be sent to each member on admission to membership and shall be delivered to any other person on demand on payment of 10p.

43. SECURITY AND INDEMNITY OF OFFICERS

(a) The Committee may require any officer having receipt or charge of money to become bound either with or without a surety as the Committee determines in a bond according to one of the

38. S.S. 45, 46.
39. S.15.

forms set out in Schedule 4 of the Act or to give the security of a guarantee society in such sum as the Committee direct conditional for rendering a just and true account of all monies received by that officer on account of the Society as a General Meeting or the Committee require, and for the payment of all sums due to the Society.

(b) Every officer shall be indemnified by the Society against all expenses and costs reasonably incurred in the discharge of that officer's duties, including travelling expenses.

44. AUDIT[40]

(a) The General Meeting shall in each year of account appoint an auditor in accordance with Section 4 of the Friendly and Industrial and Provident Societies Act 1968 to audit the Society's accounts and balance sheets for that year. The auditor shall be a person who is a qualified auditor under Section 7 of the said Act.

(b) The first auditor shall be appointed by the Committee within three months after the registration of the Society, or by a General Meeting if held within that time. The Committee may appoint an auditor to fill any casual vacancy occurring between general meetings.

(c) Subject to the provisions of Sections 5 and 6 of the said Act none of the following persons shall be appointed as auditor of the Society:

(i) an officer or servant of the Society;
(ii) a person who is a partner of or in the employment of, or who employs an officer or servant of the Society;
(iii) a body corporate;
(iv) any other person otherwise ineligible by virtue of Section 8 of the said Act.

(d) An auditor appointed to audit the accounts and balance sheets of the Society for the preceding year of account (whether appointed by the Committee or by the General Meeting) shall be re-appointed as auditor for the current year of account unless:

(i) a resolution has been passed at a general meeting of the

---

40. S.1(1)(b), para.10.

Society appointing somebody instead of that auditor or providing expressly that the auditor shall not be re-appointed; or
(ii) the auditor has given notice in writing to the Society of unwillingness to be re-appointed; or
(iii) the auditor is ineligible for appointment for the current year of account; or
(iv) the auditor has ceased so to act by reason of incapacity

Provided that a retiring auditor shall not be automatically re-appointed if notice of an intended resolution to appoint another person in his place has been given in accordance with paragraph (e) of this Rule and the resolution cannot be proceeded with because that other person is not a qualified auditor or is a person mentioned in paragraph (e) of this Rule.

(e) A resolution at a general meeting of the Society

(i) appointing another person as auditor in place of a retiring auditor or
(ii) providing expressly that a retiring auditor shall not be re-appointed

shall not be effective unless notice of the intention to move it has been given to the Society not less than 28 days before the meeting at which it is to be moved. On receipt by the Society of notice of such an intended resolution the Society shall forthwith send a copy of the notice to the retiring auditor. If it is practicable to do so the Society shall give notice to its members of the intended resolution at the same time and in the same manner as it gives notice in accordance with these Rules of the meeting at which the resolution is to be moved or, if that is not practicable, by advertisement not less than 14 days before the said meeting in a newspaper circulating in the area in which the Society conducts business. Where the retiring auditor makes any representations in writing to the Society with respect to the intended resolution or notifies the Society that he intends to make such representations the Society shall notify the members accordingly as required by Section 6 of the Friendly and Industrial and Provident Societies Act, 1968.

(f) The auditor shall in accordance with Section 9 of the said Act make a report to the Society on the accounts examined by the auditor and on the revenue account or accounts and on the balance sheet of the Society for the year of account in respect of that appointment.

(g) The auditor shall have the right of access at all times to the books, deeds and accounts of the Society, and to all other documents relating to its affairs and shall be entitled to require from the officers of the Society such information and explanations as the auditor thinks necessary for the performance of the duties of auditor.

(h) The auditor shall be entitled to attend the general meetings of the Society, and to receive all notices of and communications relating to any general meeting which any member of the Society is entitled to receive. The auditor shall be entitled to be heard at any meeting on any part of the business of the meeting which is of proper concern to an auditor.

(i) The Committee shall lay before each annual general meeting:

   (i) a revenue account and balance sheet audited and signed by the auditor and incorporating the report of the auditor thereon; and
   (ii) a report by the Committee on the position of the affairs of the Society signed by the Chairperson of the Committee at which that report is adopted

45. ANNUAL RETURN[41]

(a) Every year not later than the date prescribed by the Act, or three months after the date prescribed by the Registrar, the Secretary shall send to the Registrar the annual return, in the form prescribed by the Registrar and relating to the affairs of the Society for the last accounting year together with:

   (i) a copy of the report of the auditor on the Society's accounts for that year; and
   (ii) a copy of each balance sheet made during that period and of the auditor's report thereon.

(b) The Society shall on demand supply free of charge to any member or person with an interest in the funds of the Society a copy of the latest annual return together with a copy of the auditor's report on the accounts and balance sheet contained in the return.

(c) The Society shall at all times keep a copy of the latest balance

---

41. S.39.

sheet of the Society together with a copy of the auditor's report thereon hung up in a conspicuous place at the registered office.

46. NOMINATIONS[42]

(a) A member may nominate a person or persons to become entitled at that member's death to any of that member's property in the Society up to the amount permitted by law.

(b) A nomination shall be by written statement signed by the member and sent or delivered to the registered office. A nomination may be varied or revoked in the same way during the member's lifetime in accordance with the Act.

(c) The Society shall keep at its registered office a book in which the names of all persons so nominated and any variation or revocation of the nomination shall be recorded.

(d) On receiving satisfactory proof of the death of a member who has made a valid nomination the Committee shall at its discretion either transfer the property or pay an equivalent sum to the person or persons entitled thereto.

(e) Shares in the Society shall be cancelled on death in accordance with Rule 8(e); accordingly no shares shall pass by way of nomination.

47. DEATH OR BANKRUPTCY[43]

Upon receiving a claim from the personal representative of a deceased member or the trustee in bankruptcy of a bankrupt member to any property in the Society belonging to the deceased or bankrupt member the Committee shall transfer such property or at its discretion pay an equivalent sum to the personal representative or the trustee in bankruptcy.

48. DISSOLUTION

(a) The Society may be dissolved by the consent of three quarters of the members, testified by their signatures to an instrument of

---

42. S.1(1)(b), para.11, Ss 23,24.
43. S.1(1)(b), para.11.

dissolution in the form prescribed by the Treasury regulations; or by winding up in the manner provided by the Act.

(b) On the dissolution or winding up of the Society any surplus assets remaining after the satisfaction of all the Society's debts and liabilites (including debts and liabilites to members) shall be distributed in the following order:

(i) as provided in the instrument of dissolution or otherwise decided upon by the General Meeting;[44]
(ii) to the repayment of members' share capital;
(iii) to the payment to members of the sums standing to the credit of their reserve accounts;
(iv) to the employee members in proportion to the length of their service with the Society.[45]

(c) In the cases of (b)(iii) and (iv) above, all persons who were members within three years prior to the dissolution or winding up of the Society shall be treated as members and all transfers from reserve accounts to the general reserves of the Society within three years prior to the dissolution shall for the purpose of (b)(iii) above be reversed save that the respective figures by which their proportionate share or the sum standing to their reserve account shall be calculated shall be reduced by one third for each full year which has elapsed between their ceasing to be a member or the date of the relevant transfer and the date of dissolution or winding up.[46]

---

44. As to what beneficiaries may be included in the distribution see *In Re* Bucks Constabulary Widow's and Orphan's Fund Friendly Society, Thompson v Holdsworth and others 1978 1WLR 641.
45. If it is desired to reflect the level of salary as well as length of service the following words could be added: "multiplied by their salary at the time of dissolution or cessation of employment"
46. Shortly prior to a solvent winding up the General Meeting could cause the individual reserve accounts to be amalgamated into a general reserve. This would clearly benefit those members who had served longest in the Society or had the smallest reserve account, 48(c) ensures that this does not happen (see text p.37).

49. AMENDMENT OF RULES[47]

(a) Any of these Rules may be amended by the General Meeting with the concurring votes of not less than three quarters of those members present at the meeting in person or by proxy.

(b) At least 14 days clear notice of any general meeting called to consider an amendment of Rules shall be given to all members, such notice reciting the proposed resolution by which the amendment is to be made.

(c) No amendment to these Rules shall be valid until registered in accordance with the Act.

---

47. S.1(1)(b), para.5. It may prove useful to change the Rules as the Society progresses and experience shows that particular Rules are otiose, cumbersome or lacking. The proportion required to change the Rules is not fixed by Statute. Further, the Rules might provide for different proportions for different rule amendments. In general, a three quarters majority is an appropriate figure which balances flexibility with protection of minorities. The Registrar will however refuse to register an amendment if it is contrary to the statutory requirements for a Society. Further, it would appear that the only amendments which may validly be made (whether or not they are registered) are those which may reasonably be considered to have been in the contemplation of its members when the Society was formed. Any amendment must be made bona fide and must not be inconsistent with the nature of the Society.

THE COMPANIES ACT 1985

Worker Controlled Private Company Limited by Shares
MEMORANDUM OF ASSOCIATION of
Limited.

1. The name of the Company is   Limited.

2. The registered office of the Company will be situate in England [Wales].

3. The objects for which the company is established are:

(A) to carry on as a worker controlled company the business of..........
[insert main objects clause];

(B) to establish and promote the holding of shares in the Company by or on behalf of its employees (which for the purpose of this Memorandum shall include the employees of any subsidiary of the Company) whether by a scheme recognised by statute or otherwise;

(C) to make gifts to or enter into any arrangement with any person or provide assistance of any sort for the purpose of assisting employees of the Company to acquire shares in and control of the Company or for the purpose of assisting or enabling trustees of any trust established for the benefit of the employees or former employees (or such employees as are or were members of the Company) or their relatives or dependants or for any other trust which satisfies the requirements of Section 86 of the Inheritance Tax Act 1984 or any statutory modification, amendment or re-enactment thereof to acquire shares in the Company;

(D) to carry on any other business which may in the opinion of the Company in general meeting of the Company be conveniently carried on by the Company in connection with or in furtherance of any of its objects;

(E) to purchase, take on lease or in exchange, hire and otherwise acquire any land, buildings, easements, machinery, plant, vehicles and stock in trade, and any other real and personal property, rights or privileges whatsoever which the Company may think necessary or convenient for the purpose of its business, and to let out, license, or otherwise dispose of such part of such property as may not be immediately required for the principal business of the Company;

(F) to apply for, purchase, or otherwise acquire, and protect and renew in any part of the world any patents, patent rights, trade marks, designs, licenses, concessions, and the like, conferring any exclusive or non-exclusive or limited right to their use, or any secret or other information relating to any of the purposes of the Company, or the acquisition of which may seem calculated directly or indirectly to benefit the Company, and to use, exercise, develop, or grant licences in respect of, or otherwise turn to account the property, rights or information so acquired;

(G) to build, construct, alter, maintain, enlarge, pull down, remove or replace, and to work, manage and control any buildings, offices, factories, shops, machinery, engines, roads, ways, railways, branches or sidings, bridges, reservoirs, watercourses, wharves, electric works and other works and conveniences which may seem calculated directly or indirectly to advance the interests of the Company, and to join with any other person or company in doing any of these things;

(H) to acquire and undertake the whole or any part of the business, property, and liabilities of any person or company carrying on or proposing to carry on any business which the Company is authorised to carry on, or possessed of property suitable for the purposes of the Company, or which can be carried on in conjunction therewith or which is capable of being conducted so as directly or indirectly to benefit the Company or its employees;

(I) to subscribe for, take, or otherwise acquire, and hold shares, debentures, or other securities of any other company having objects altogether or in part similar to those of the Company, or carrying on any business capable of being conducted so as directly or indirectly to benefit the Company or its employees and to establish or promote any company or companies for the purpose of acquiring all or any of the property, rights and liabilities of the Company or for any other purpose which may seem directly or indirectly calculated to benefit the Company or its employees and to place or guarantee the placing of, underwrite, subscribe for or otherwise acquire all or any part of the shares, debentures or other securities of any such other company;

(J) to amalgamate or enter into partnership or into any arrangement for sharing of profits, union of interest, co-operation, joint adventure, reciprocal concession, or otherwise, with any person or company carrying on or engaged in or about to carry on or engage in any business or transaction which the company is authorised to carry on or engage in, or any business or transaction capable of being conducted so as directly or indirectly to benefit the Company or its employees;

(K) to enter into any arrangements with any government or authority, supreme, municipal, local or otherwise, that may seem conducive to the Company's objects, or any of them, and to obtain from any such government or authority any rights, privileges and concessions which the Company may think it desirable to obtain, and to carry out, exercise, and comply with any such arrangements, rights, privileges, and concessions;

(L) to apply for, promote and obtain any Act of Parliament, charter, privilege, concession, licence or authorisation of any government, state or municipality, provisional order or licence of the Department of Trade or other authority for enabling the Company to carry any of its objects into effect or for extending any of the powers of the Company or for effecting any modification of the constitution of the Company, for furthering the co-operative or common ownership movements, or for any other purpose which may seem expedient, to oppose any proceedings or applications which may seem calculated directly or indirectly to prejudice the interests of the Company, and to take any proceedings in any court for relief whether declaratory or otherwise which may seem expedient;

(M) to pay for any rights or property acquired by or for any services rendered to the Company, and subject to the Articles of Association of the Company to remunerate any person or company whether by cash payment or by the allotment of shares, debentures or other securities in the Company credited as paid up in full or in part or otherwise;

(N) to receive money on deposit or loan and borrow or raise money in such manner as the Company shall think fit, and in particular by the issue of debentures, or debenture stock (perpetual or otherwise) and to secure the repayment of any money borrowed, raised or owing by mortgage, charge or lien upon all or any of the property or assets of the company (both present and future) including its uncalled capital, and also by a similar mortgage, charge or lien to secure and guarantee the performance by the Company or any other person or company of any obligation undertaken by the Company or any other person or company as the case may be;

(O) to invest and deal with the moneys of the Company not immediately required in any manner and to lend and advance money or give credit to such persons or companies and on such terms as may seem expedient, and in particular to customers and others having dealings with the Company, or on terms less favourable than might otherwise be obtained to other worker controlled or common ownership corporations and to guarantee the performance of any contract or obligation and the payment of money of or by any such persons or companies;

(P) to draw, make, accept, indorse, discount, execute, and issue promisory notes, bills of exchange, bills of lading, warrants, debentures, and other negotiable or transferable instruments;

(Q) to establish and maintain or procure the establishment and maintenance of any contributory or non-contributory pension or superannuation funds for the benefit of, and give or procure the giving of donations, gratuities, pensions, allowances, bonuses or payments of any kind whatsoever to any persons who are or were at any time employees of the Company or who are or were at any time Directors or officers of the Company or of any such other company as aforesaid, and the spouses, ex-spouses, families and dependants of any such persons, and make payments to or towards the insurance of any such person as aforesaid;

(R) to establish and support or aid in the establishment and support of associations, institutions, funds, trusts, and conveniences calculated to benefit employees or directors or past employees or directors of the Company or of its predecessors in business, or the dependants or connections of any such persons, or the co-operative or common ownership movements;

(S) to subscribe or guarantee money for charitable or benevolent objects, or for any exhibition, or for any public, general, or useful object;

(T) to pay out of the funds of the Company all expenses which the Company may lawfully pay with respect to the formation and registration of the Company or the issue of its capital, including brokerage and commissions for obtaining applications for or taking, placing or under-writing or procuring the underwriting of shares, debentures or other securities of the Company;

(U) to sell, lease, mortgage or otherwise dispose of the property, assets or undertaking of the Company or any part thereof for such consideration as the Company may think fit, and in particular for shares, stock, debentures, or other securities of any other company, whether or not having objects altogether or in part similar to those of the Company;

(V) to distribute among the member in specie any property of the Company, or any proceeds of sale or disposal of any property of the Company, but so that no distribution amounting to a reduction of capital be made except with the sanction (if any) for the time being required by law and such that no distribution to employee shareholders shall be made by reference to the level of such members' shareholdings;

(W) to make provision in connection with the cessation or the transfer to any person of the whole or part of the undertaking of the Company or any subsidiary of the Company for the benefit of persons employed or formerly employed by the Company or that subsidiary with the sanction of any ordinary resolution of the Company or a resolution of the Directors;

(X) to act as agents or brokers and as trustees for any person or company and to undertake and perform sub-contracts and to do all or any of the above things in any part of the world, and either as principals, agents, trustees, contractors or otherwise, and either alone or jointly with others, and either by or through agents, sub-contractors, trustees or otherwise;

(Y) to do all such other things as may appear to the Company to be incidental or conductive to the attainment of the above objects or any of them.

AND IT IS HEREBY DECLARED THAT:

(a) the word "company" in this clause, except where used in reference to this Company, shall be deemed to include any industrial and provident society, partnership or other body of persons, whether corporate or unincorporate, and whether domiciled in the United Kingdom or elsewhere, and

(b) the objects set forth in any sub-clause of this clause shall not be restrictively construed but the widest interpretations shall be given to them, and they shall not, except when the context expressly so requires, be in any way limited to or restricted by reference to or inference from any other object or objects set forth in such sub-clause or from the terms of any other sub-clause or by the name of the Company, save that the objects shall be construed in a manner consistent with the Company existing as a Company controlled by its employees.

4. The liability of the members is limited.

5. The Company's share capital is £   divided into   shares of £   each. The share capital of the Company may be increased or reduced by any means lawful and in accordance with its regulations, may be divided into separate classes and may have attached thereto whether on issue or subsequently such rights and restrictions as to dividend, capital,

voting or otherwise as the Company shall in accordance with its regulations decide.

WE, the Subscribers to this Memorandum of Association, wish to be formed into a Company in pursuance of this Memorandum. We each agree to take the number of shares shown opposite our respective names.

NAMES AND ADDRESSES OF SUBSCRIBERS	NUMBER OF SHARES TAKEN

[at least two persons must subscribe to the memorandum]

	Total shares taken

DATED this   day of

Witness to the above signatures

THE COMPANIES ACT 1985

Worker Controlled Private Company Limited by Shares

ARTICLES OF ASSOCIATION OF
Limited

(Table A referred to below published by HM Stationery Office, is set out in full in the Appendix).

PRELIMINARY

1. The regulations contained in Table A in the Companies (Tables A to F) Regulations 1985 ("Table A") shall apply to the Company subject to the following exclusions and modifications. Regulations 8, 24, 37, 40, 41, 46, 54, 59, 73 to 80, 88, 89 and 109 shall not apply to the Company.

PRIVATE COMPANY

2. The Company is a private company and save to the extent permitted by Section 170(2) of the Financial Services Act 1986 the Company shall not issue or cause to be issued in the United Kingdom an advertisement offering securities to be issued by the Company.

SHARES

3. (a) At the date of the adoption of these Articles the share capital of the Company is £   divided into   shares of £1 each. The share capital of the Company shall be issued as one of two classes of shares, namely Employee Shares and Investor Shares.

(b) The shares of the Company shall be under the control of the directors. The directors of the Company may, subject to these Articles, within a period of five years from the date of incorporation of the Company exercise the Company's power to allot, grant options over or otherwise dispose of all or any relevant securities in the capital of the Company within the meaning of Section 80(2) of the Act unissued at the date of the adoption of this article[1].

4. Sections 89(1) and 90(1) to (6) of the Act shall not apply to the Company[2].

EMPLOYEE SHARES

5. No Employee Share in the Company shall be issued or transferred to any person other than an employee of the Company or an employee of a subsidiary of the Company or to a trustee or trustees as provided in Article 14. No Employee Share shall be issued other than as a fully paid share.

ENTITLEMENT OF EMPLOYEE TO BECOME A MEMBER

6. The Company in general meeting may make rules from time to time determining the necessary qualifications required for any employee to become a member ("the Rules"). Such qualifications may include requirements for minimum length of service with the Company, minimum hours worked per week, requirements for the purchase of certain quantities of shares in the Company or the maintenance of a loan or reserve account with the Company or such other conditions as the Company thinks fit. The Rules shall not require that an employee be employed for a period exceeding [six] months, nor work more than [twenty] hours per week, [nor contribute a sum exceeding [20] per cent of that employee's gross salary by way of share purchase loan or reserve account].[3]

7. The directors shall[4] allot Employee Shares in the Company to any person qualified to hold such shares under Articles 5 and 6 above who:

1. Companies Act 1985 Section 80. The directors of the Company must be authorised to allot shares. The general authority given here is the maximum permissible both in terms of time and amount of shares. The authority must be renewed after five years or it will lapse. If it is desired to keep the issue of new shares more closely in the hands of the general meeting this sub-rule may be deleted. This authority is not necessary in the case of shares issued pursuant to an employee share scheme.
2. This provision disapplies the statutory pre-emption provisions which require that new shares are offered to existing shareholders pro-rata. This is clearly not appropriate in a co-operative company.
3. The Rules should not impose artificial restrictions on entry designed to enhance the value of the existing members' shares in the Company. When deciding upon the relevant limits account should be taken of possible part-time or work-sharing employees.
4. It may be that the members of the Company wish to have an individual say in the identity of other members. If not all the members are directors of the Company the article could provide for the prior sanction of the general meeting. However, if a person is to remain as an employee they should be admitted to membership.

(i) makes application for such shares, and
(ii) tenders to the directors the necessary sums required to pay up the said shares and comply with any of the financial conditions imposed by the Rules

save that the directors shall not be obliged to allot to such person more than one share or, if greater, the minimum number of shares required to be held under the Rules.

INVESTOR SHARES

8. The directors may with the sanction of the Company in General Meeting allot Investor Shares to such persons [other than employees][5] as the directors may think fit. Investor Shares may be issued with such special, deferred or preferential rights as the directors may decide upon, and may be issued as one or more classes of shares, but the rights attached thereto shall not in any case exceed those permitted to Investor Shares under these articles. Investor Shares shall carry no right to receive notice of or attend and vote at any general meeting of the Company.[6]

LIEN

9. In addition to the lien conferred by regulation 8 of Table A the Company shall have such a lien on all shares registered in the name of any member whether solely or as one of joint holders for all monies presently payable by that member or that member's estate to the Company on any account.

TRANSFER OF SHARES

10. Any member may transfer shares to a person already holding shares of that class provided that:
(i) no Employee Share shall be transferred to a person who is not an existing employee of the Company or its subsidiary, and
(ii) no transfer of an Employee Share shall be registered which would have the effect of reducing any person's shareholding to below the minimum required by the Rules (unless the

5. There is no reason why, on the face of it, employees should not also hold investor shares. It may be desired to arrange with an investing institution that such shares are used in a profit sharing scheme (see page 76) in which case these words should be omitted. However, this would break down the principle of members receiving rewards measured by reference to their participation in the Company. See also clause 3(v) of the memorandum.
6. Investor shares will primarily be aimed at institutions, and it will be a matter of negotiation in each case what rights are given to them. It is likely that such rights will ensure the investor a preferential dividend and return on a winding up.

transfer is of the whole of that person's shareholding);

(iii) no Employee Share shall be transferred without the consent of the directors if that transfer would have the effect of increasing any person's shareholding to above such amount (if any) as has been decided by the Company in general meeting on the maximum preferred level of shareholding.

11. No Employee Share shall be transferred to any person who is not an existing member of the Company unless
 (i) that person is qualified to be a member under the Rules, and
 (ii) the transfer is approved by the directors.[7]

12. Save as aforesaid, the directors may, in their absolute discretion and without assigning any reason therefor, decline to register any transfer of any share.[8]

TRANSFER ON CESSATION OF EMPLOYMENT

13. (a) When the holder of an Employee Share ceases to be employed by the Company for whatever reason (including dismissal by the Company or death) the directors may at any time thereafter give notice to that member (which for this Article shall include that member's personal representative) requiring that the member transfer their entire shareholding in the Company within the succeeding period of twenty eight days to such person or persons as the directors shall nominate.[9]

(b) If a notice under clause (a) above shall not be complied with the directors may at any time thereafter by resolution authorise some person to transfer such shares to the person or persons to whom the shares are required to be transferred. The transferee of any share so transferred shall thereupon be registered as the holder of the share and shall not be bound to see to the application of the purchase money, if any, nor shall that person's title to the share be affected by any irregularity or invalidity in the proceedings in reference to the disposal of the share. Any person

---

7. The directors may conveniently approve the transfer of shares from a retiring employee to that person's replacement. The same considerations of approval of the general meeting apply as for the allotment of shares.
8. Investors may require that shares issued to them are transferable, in which case this provision must be altered.
9. The ideal candidate would be a new employee member who would be able to provide the funds. Alternatively the trustees of an employee trust would be well placed to "soak up" excess shares. If necessary the Company could buy the shares or give assistance for their purchase under the provisions of the Companies Act. Although the shares lose their right to vote, they still rank for any dividend paid on employee shares. It would be possible to provide that on cessation of employment a member is no longer entitled to rank for dividend, but this has not been done in the present draft.

whose share has been transferred in accordance with this Article shall forthwith deliver up to the Company the share certificate (if any) issued to them in respect of that share.

(c) The holder of any share transferred in accordance with 13(b) above shall be entitled to receive from the transferee the nominal amount paid up on such share and no more, save that if the directors are of the opinion that the net asset value of the share is less than par the directors may instruct the Company's auditors (acting as experts and not as arbitrators) to value the share on a net asset basis. If the net asset value is less than par, but not otherwise, the net asset value shall be the price for that share.

EMPLOYEE TRUST

14. Notwithstanding Articles 6, 10 and 11 any share may be issued or transferred to the trustees of a trust approved by the Company in general meeting established for the benefit of the employees or former employees (or such employees as are or were members of the Company) or their relatives or dependants or, if such trusts satisfy the requirements of Section 86 of the Inheritance Tax Act 1984 or any statutory modification, amendment or re-enactment thereof, for any other beneficiaries.[10]

GENERAL MEETINGS

15. Any director and any two[11] or more holders of employee shares may call a general meeting of the Company. Notices of a general meeting need only be sent to those persons qualified to vote at such meeting in accordance with Article 18.

QUORUM

16. No business shall be transacted at any meeting unless a quorum is present at the time the meeting proceeds to business. A quorum shall be present if at least three quarters of the employee members are present in person, or by proxy.[12]

10. A trust so established should be able to take advantage of the taxation benefits available. One or more trusts (administered by the same trustees) might be established.
11. Under the Act members holding one tenth of the paid up share capital may call a general meeting. For alternative provision see Society Rule No.15.
12. This provision is important. We have provided for a large quorum to ensure that the Company is in practice as well as in theory controlled by its employee members. If this figure is likely to prove impractical it should be reduced, alternatively a definite number substituted. As drafted, Article 17 ensures that business can be carried out at an adjourned meeting with a smaller quorum (two) if the first meeting is inquorate.

17. If a quorum is not present within half an hour from the time appointed for the meeting the meeting shall be adjourned to the same day in the next week at the same time and place or to such other time and place as the directors may determine. If adjourned to some other time and place notice of such adjournment shall be given to the members. At such adjourned meeting the employee members present shall constitute a quorum.

VOTING

18. At any meeting of the company the only persons qualified to vote on any resolution shall be those members who are the existing employees of the company. On a show of hands every employee member who is present in person shall have one vote, and on a poll every employee member shall have one vote regardless of the number of shares held by that member.[13]

PROXIES

19. On a poll votes may be given either personally or by proxy.

20. An instrument appointing a proxy and any necessary authorities shall be valid if deposited at the relevant place not less than 24 hours prior to the meeting, but the directors may in their discretion admit a form of proxy at any time and shall admit such form if satisfied that the proxy would (had it been delivered more than 24 hours prior to the meeting) otherwise have been valid. Regulation 62 of Table A shall be modified accordingly.[14]

DIRECTORS

21. A director shall not be required to be a member of the Company but no person shall be appointed a director if such appointment would cause the number of non-employee directors to exceed the number of directors who are employed by the Company.[15]

---

13. This is the essence of the co-operative structure of the company. Every employee member will have one vote irrespective of their capital contribution to the Company, their salary, or any other matter.
14. To encourage participation in decision making it is desirable that there should be few restrictions on voting. Nevertheless, some degree of certainty is desirable to avoid unnecessary disputes.
15. It would be a simple matter to provide that only employee members may be directors. This may however deny the Company the experience and advice of non-members which might prove valuable. Accordingly provisions have been built into the articles to ensure that the non-employee directors do not have control.

22. (a) All the directors of the Company shall retire at the end of each Annual General Meeting of the Company but shall be eligible for re-election.[16]

(b) If at the Annual General Meeting of the Company no resolution is proposed to appoint or re-appoint any directors of the Company the retiring directors shall be taken to have stood for re-election and shall be deemed to have been duly re-elected.

(c) In addition to the powers of removal and appointment given by these Articles or by the Act, a director may be appointed or removed by ordinary resolution.

(d) A person who is not both a member of the Company and employed by the Company may only stand for election to the office of director if nominated by a member. The nomination shall be in writing, signed by the member and containing a signed statement by the person nominated of willingness to act. The nomination shall be delivered to the registered office not less than 7 days prior to the meeting. Such a person once duly elected a director may stand for re-election without further nomination.

23. No director who is also an employee of the Company may be remunerated for duties carried out as a director (but may receive remuneration as an employee or for other services of value provided to the Company). Regulation 82 of Table A shall be modified accordingly.[17]

APPOINTMENTS AND PENSIONS OF DIRECTORS

24. The Company in general meeting (to the exclusion of the directors) shall exercise the powers given by regulations 84 and 87 and 99 of Table A which shall be modified accordingly. The last sentence of regulation 84 of Table A shall not apply to the Company.[18]

16. If the membership is small it may be practicable (it is certainly desirable) for all members to be directors. The only limit is the size of the board as a unit for making swift decisions, although this can be overcome to some extent by the use of committees of the directors. If this is the wish the retirement provisions can be replaced with a provision that each member is entitled to be appointed a director, but this is not essential as the retiring directors will in any event be deemed to have been re-elected if no new resolution is proposed at each annual general meeting. If it is desired to appoint the board of directors by proportional representation see the suggested clause in the note to Society Rule 25 which could be adapted and added to this sub-clause.
17. The basis of employee control is that the employees manage the Company. It does not seem appropriate to give those persons who act as directors any more remuneration for doing what is, in an employee controlled company, no more than their job. This provision would also prevent "competition" for directorships based upon financial gain.

25. A director may vote as a director and may be counted for the purpose of a quorum in regard to any contract or arrangement in which that person is interested, or upon any matter arising from such contract or arrangement provided that that person has disclosed the full nature of that interest to the meeting at which such vote is taken.[19]

PROCEEDINGS OF DIRECTORS

26. The directors shall meet as often as is required for the proper conduct of the Company's business and in any case at least once [a week].[20] A director may, and the secretary at the request of a director shall, call a meeting of the directors. It shall not be necessary to give notice of a meeting to a director who is absent from the United Kingdom.

VOTING

27. Any questions arising for decision at a meeting of the directors shall be decided by simple majority. In the case of an equality of votes the votes of non-employees of the Company shall be discounted to obtain a result. If there still remains an equality of votes the Chairperson shall have a second or casting vote, or shall be entitled to convene a general meeting for the purpose of deciding that question.[21]

QUORUM

28. The quorum for a meeting of the directors shall be [three] but at a meeting where less than half the directors present are employees of the Company no business shall be transacted save

---

18. It seems appropriate, for the reasons given in the previous footnote, to give the company in general meeting the power to decide directly upon benefits given to officers of the Company. However, the directors will, as the articles stand, have the power to appoint and pay new employees.
19. For alternative provisions see Society Rule No.28.
20. The frequency of directors' meetings will depend upon a great many factors. Although no provision has been made for the frequency of general meetings (other than annual general meetings) the entire employee membership should also meet with reasonable frequency. The important factor is that the direction of the Company is not left to one small group of people for any great length of time.
21. This article should, together with the quorum provisions, provide for a method of decision making where the employee directors will never be in a minority. The Article provides for the Chairperson to have a casting vote. This can be excluded if so desired, but it does provide for certainty. If decisions are taken by consensus rather than by counting votes the use of the casting vote will be kept to a minimum.

that of adjourning the meeting, or convening a general meeting of the Company.[22]

BORROWING — THE PRESCRIBED RATE

29. (a) The directors shall exercise all of the powers of the Company to borrow money. Such power shall be unlimited unless previously limited by the Company in general meeting, but no person dealing with the Company in good faith shall be bound to inquire into whether such a limit has been set.

(b) The Company shall not take deposits but may borrow from its members.

(c) The Company shall not pay interest on any loan from its employee members at a rate exceeding 3 per cent above the base lending rate of [the Co-operative Bank Plc] or 10 per cent per annum, whichever is the higher ("The prescribed rate").[23]

MEMBERS' LOAN ACCOUNTS

30. The Company shall keep an account of all sums received from members or credited as received from members by way of loan. The members' loan acounts shall carry simple interest from year to year at such rate (if any) as may be decided by the Company in general meeting from time to time. Such rate shall not exceed the prescribed rate. The terms of repayment of loan accounts shall be determined by the Company but in default of such determination the loan shall be repayable on notice by the Company, or within six months of the date of a written demand from the member to the Company.[24]

MEMBERS' RESERVE ACCOUNTS

31. The Company shall keep accounts called "members' reserve accounts" recording all retained profits credited to members' reserve accounts and sums received from members or credited as

22. The quorum might be higher, and in a small Company where each employeee member is a director, could be the same as for a quorum at a general meeting.
23. The intention is to ensure that the members do not lend to the Company with a view to making a profit on their lending. Nevertheless they may receive a reasonable rate of return sufficient to encourage them to maintain loan accounts (where not compelled to do so by the Rules). A company has greater flexibility than a society in fixing the rate of interest as it is not bound by any Registrar's ruling as is a society, see p.87.
24. The Company will wish to have as long as is possible to repay the loan, particularly when cash flow is restricted. The terms of the loan must ensure that a dissentient member cannot simply demand the repayment of their loan, thereby precipitating the winding up of the Company.

received from members by way of contribution to the Company other than sums received by way of loan or as payment for shares. Such sums shall be the absolute property of the Company and may if the directors think fit and the Company in general meeting approves be transferred in whole or in part to general reserves.

32. The directors shall recommend what proportion of retained profit, including unrealised profit is available for credit to members' reserve accounts. The provisions of Article 37(c) shall apply to transactions under this article as if sums to be credited to members' reserve accounts were profits to be distributed.[25]

33. The Company may, in accordance with Article 37, pay dividends to members calculated by reference to their respective reserve accounts. No dividend shall be paid on any sum standing to the credit of a member's reserve account at a rate exceeding the prescribed rate.[26]

34. On cessation of employment of a member, the Company:
 (i) may take into account the amount standing to the credit of a member's reserve account in deciding what sum, if any, to pay to that member as compensation for loss of office, or as a gratuity, (and in such a case shall debit that member's reserve account by such sum), or
 (ii) may in general meeting, subject to the Act and the rights of the holders of Investor Shares declare a dividend of such sum as may lawfully be distributed standing to the credit of such reserve account to the retiring member without declaring a dividend to any other member;
but no member shall upon ceasing employment have any right to any such payment and except as provided in Article 40 (Winding Up) shall have no claim to any sum standing to their reserve account. On cessation of membership any sum standing to the credit of a person's reserve account shall be transferred to the general reserve.

APPLICATION OF PROFITS

35. The directors shall recommend what profit if any is available for distribution in any year. Such profit as is not distributed shall be retained in a general or in members' reserve accounts but any sums standing to the credit of the general reserve or members' reserve accounts and representing distributable profit for that or

25. This gives the directors the ability to adjust the levels of reserve accounts on an individual basis.
26. The prescribed rate is defined in Article 29(c).

previous years may be applied as profit in any subsequent year in accordance with the Act and these Articles. If recommended by the directors and approved by the Company in general meeting the reserves of the Company available for distribution may be applied in paying up bonus shares to be issued to trustees of a trust approved under Article 14 whether or not such trustees are existing members of the Company.

36. The Company may by ordinary resolution declare that dividends be paid to the holders of Investor Shares in accordance with the respective rights attached thereto.

37. (a) The profits of the Society not retained and not distributed to the holders of Investor Shares in accordance with the rights attached thereto shall be applied as follows in such manner and in such proportion as is recommended by the directors and approved by the Company in general meeting. Profits available for distribution may be applied in:
   (i) the payment of dividends on Employee Shares at a rate not exceeding the prescribed rate;[26]
   (ii) the payment of interest on members' reserve accounts at a rate not exceeding the prescribed rate;[26]
   (iii) the payment to employee members of bonus payments in such proportion as decided by the Company in general meeting and which is related to their participation in the Company, but not to their shareholding.[27]

   (b) Payment shall be by way of:
   (i) cash distribution;
   (ii) credit to a member's loan account; or
   (iii) the allocation of bonus shares treated as paid up to a member or to trustees qualified under Article 14 to be members.

   (c) If authorised by the Company in general meeting to carry out any policy of the Company with regard to members holding particular sums in loan account or with regard to the preferred level of shareholding of each member, the directors shall have the power to allocate each member's share of distributed profit on an individual basis in such manner as they think fit in order to comply with such policies.

ACCOUNTS

38. Any member shall have the right to inspect the accounting

[27] The members may wish to make bonus payments equally to all members or according to salary or earnings or according to some other formula reflecting their participation in the Company.

records or other books or documents of the Company unless otherwise agreed by the Company in general meeting.[28]

ARTICLES

39. Every member, upon first becoming the holder of any Employee Share shall be entitled without payment to a copy of these Articles and a copy of the relevant Table A. It shall be the duty of the Secretary to ensure that each member has received such copies.

WINDING UP

40. (a) On the winding up of the Company any surplus assets remaining after the satisfaction of all the Company's debts and liabilities (including debts and liabilities to members) shall be distributed in the following order:
   (i) as required by the terms of issue of the Investor Shares;
   (ii) to the payment to members of the nominal sum paid up on the members' share capital;
   (iii) as decided upon by extraordinary resolution of the Company in general meeting;
   (iv) to the payment to members of the sums standing to the credit of their reserve account;
   (v) to the members employed by the Company on the date of the winding up in proportion to the length of their service with the Society.[29]

(b) In the case of (iv) above all sums transferred from members' reserve accounts to the general reserves of the Company within the previous three years shall be treated as re-transferred to the members' reserve accounts save that the nominal sums re-transferred shall be reduced by one third for each full year which has elapsed between the date of the original transfer and the date of winding up.

(c) In the case of (v) above all persons who were employee members within three years prior to the winding up of the Company shall be treated as members employed at the date of the winding up save that the respective figures by which their proportionate share shall be calculated shall be reduced by one third for each full year which has elapsed between their ceasing to be an employee and the date of winding up.

---

28. This provision goes beyond the general rights of members at law. Directors do, at law, have such a power and in a worker controlled environment it is not appropriate for the directors to have any information which is denied to the employee members.
29. If it is desired to reflect the level of salary as well as length of service this sub-clause should continue as follows: "multiplied by their salary at the time of dissolution or cessation of employment".

SETTLEMENT I

Employee Trust Settlement for Capitalising Reserves

(see text, p.40)

THIS SETTLEMENT is made the   day of   19   BETWEEN YZ LIMITED whose registered office is at [address] (hereinafter called "the Company") of the one part and AB of [address] and CD of [address] (hereinafter called "the Original Trustees") of the other part

W H E R E A S :-

(A) The Company was incorporated on [date] with limited liability under the Companies Act 1985 and has an authorised share capital of £   ;
(B) The Company carries on the business of [description of the Company's business];
(C) By a resolution dated   the Company approved the decision by [state body properly authorised by Articles] to issue fully paid up shares by way of capitalisation of profits and to transfer those shares to the trustees hereof for the benefit of the staff of the Company and their relations and dependants;[1]

---

1. Unless the Articles otherwise provide, a Company has no power to pay dividends otherwise than in cash. Table A, however, gives the directors on the authority of any ordinary resolution power to capitalise profits and distribute them as fully or partly paid shares — see Article 110. In each case, reference should be made to the Articles of the particular company. The Articles of Association above give the Company power to issue fully paid up bonus shares directly to trustees of employee trust settlements without the requirement that such trustees be already members of the Comapny — see Article 35. Although it is necessary that the existing members should approve the issue, it is considered that the issue will not constitute "a disposal by way of gift" by each individual member - see Finance Act 1986, S.102. Consequently, although the existing members will be objects of the discretionary trust, the bonus shares will not be "property subject to a reservation" — Finance Act 1986 S.102(2). To the extent that the bonus issue involves a transfer of value by the Company (which in any event is doubtful, see text), it will qualify as an exempt transfer — ITA 1984 S.13. However, there

Model Forms or Precedents

(D) The terms of this Trust Deed have been approved by the Company in general meeting by a resolution dated   ;
(E) The Company has transferred into the joint names of the Original Trustees the said shares to be held upon the trusts hereof.

NOW THIS DEED WITNESSETH as follows:

1. In this Deed unless the context otherwise requires the following terms shall have the following meanings:
(1) "the Trustees" means the Original Trustees and either the trustees or trustee for the time being hereof;
(2) "employee" means any person who at any time before the Vesting Day is employed by or holds office with the Company or any subsidiary of the Company;
(3) "beneficiary" means any Employee or former Employee any spouse child or remoter issue (including for the avoidance of doubt any adopted child) and any person who in the opinion of the trustees is a dependant of any such Employee or former Employee and Beneficiaries shall be construed accordingly;[2]
(4) "the Trust Fund" means:
  (i) the shares as are more particularly set out in Schedule I hereto (hereinafter called "the Shares")

is a risk that the Revenue will argue that each member is a "settlor" of a proportionate part of the bonus shares for income tax purposes - *see* Taxes Act 1970 Ss.448-452. However, unless the members are themselves higher rate taxpayers, it will not be in the Revenue's interest to take such a point since the income of the fund to the extent it is not distributed will be taxed at a rate of 45% and in most circumstances the amounts of income are likely to be quite small. In some circumstances, however, where the bonus issue will involve the capitalisation of large sums of retained profit, it may be advisable to keep the amount of any preferential dividend reasonably low; alternatively it would be open for the directors or equivalent body to pass the dividend in most years.
2. If the members wish to include charities as primary objects of the trusts along with current and former employees and their families, the following sub-clause should be substituted:

"(3) 'Beneficiary' means:

  (i) any Employee ... [same as Cl.1(3) of main text excluding the words '... and Beneficiaries shall be construed accordingly']
  (ii) such one or more bodies which are established for purposes which are exclusively charitable according to the law of England and Wales as the Trustees shall think fit. [Alternatively paragraph (ii) may be limited to certain named charities or the promotion of certain charitable objects] and Beneficiaries shall be construed accordingly".

(ii) all property accepted by the Trustees as additions to the Trust Fund; and

(iii) all monies investments and property from time to time representing such Shares and additions and any accumulations of income thereof;

(5) "the Vesting Day" means the day on which shall expire the period of[3] [   ] from the date of the execution of this Deed (which period shall be the Perpetuity Period applicable hereto);

(6) "Excluded Person" means any person falling within Section 13(2) (and not within Section 13(3)) of the Inheritance Tax Act 1984 as amended and in force at the execution of this Deed;[10]

(7) "subsidiary" has the same meaning as in the Companies Act 1985.

2. [The Trustees shall stand possessed of the Trust Fund and the income thereof upon such trusts for the benefit of all or such one or more exclusive of the other or others of the Beneficiaries in such shares and proportions and subject to such terms and limitations as the Trustees shall from time to time [but not before the   day of   ] by Deed or Deeds revocable or irrevocable executed before the Vesting Day but without infringing the rules against perpetuity appoint.[4]]

3. (1) [In default of and subject to any such appointment as aforesaid] the Trustees [shall stand possessed of the Trust Fund and the income thereof until the Vesting Day upon Trust to][5]

3. The perpetuity period may be for any fixed period not exceeding eighty years. It may be decided to add after "this Deed" the following: "or the date twelve months after the Company is wound up if earlier".

4. The power to appoint capital amongst the Beneficiaries at any time, although optional, gives the Trustees the necessary flexibility to deal with the different situations which may arise during the continuation of the trust. It would be unwise not to have a power exercisable over capital prior to Vesting Day unless the trust period was intended to be very short. If the members are unwilling to contemplate even the possibility of distribution of capital within a certain period, a possible compromise is to make the power under Clause 2 exercisable only after the expiration of that period.

Distributions of capital during the trust period will normally not incur any liability to Inheritance Tax. There will, however, be a charge to tax in the following circumstances:

(i) where the company is a "close company" and the payment is made to a participator who owns or is entitled to acquire five per cent or more of the shares or would be entitled on a winding up to five per cent of the assets or any person connected with him — Ss.72(2), 72(3)(b). It should be noted that by virtue of Clause 7 of this precedent payments of capital which would give rise to a charge under this head are expressly prohibited and in the absence of such prohibition any transfer of value made by the existing members would not [shall] pay or apply the income thereof within 12 months of its coming into their possession to or for the benefit of all or such one or more exclusive of the other or others of the Beneficiaries as shall be living [or in existence] for the time being in such shares as they shall in their absolute discretion think fit and subject thereto to such Beneficiaries who are or have been Employees as shall then be living in equal shares absolutely.

(2) Provided always that during the period of 21 years from the date hereof[6] the Trustees shall have power instead of dealing with the income under sub-clause (1) of this Clause to accumulate income by capitalising it as an accretion to and part of the Trust Fund.

4. (1) The Trustees shall stand possessed of the Trust Fund on the Vesting Day (subject to any appointment made in the exercise of such power as aforesaid) In Trust as to income and capital for such Beneficiaries as shall then be living [or in existence] or any one or more of them and in such shares as the Trustees shall prior to or upon the Vesting Day determine and in default of any such determination in trust for the Company absolutely.[7]

> qualify for exemption under S.13 of the Inheritance Tax Act 1984. However, S.72 deals with other employee settlements which do not seek to qualify for exemption under S.13 or S.28. Clearly if it is intended to make payments of capital to such persons either during the trust period or on its termination clauses 1(b) and 7 should be deleted, *or*
> (ii) where a payment is made to a person (or any person connected with him) who has directly or indirectly contributed property to the trust of more than £1000 in any one year of assessment. The Revenue may argue that each member who approved the bonus issue has indirectly contributed a pro rata share of the settled property. Therefore, care should be taken that this share does not exceed £1000 in any year. As a technical matter, the exception from charge applies only to people who have made contributions of less than £1000 *by way of additions* to the Trust Fund. Where it is anticipated that considerable capital distributions will be made by the trust to existing members, it would be advisable to set up the Trust Fund with a small cash payment so as to make the bonus issue an addition to the Trust Fund — S.72(3)(a).
> 5. If it is decided to do without the power in Clause 2 altogether, the bracketed provision should be inserted as indicated:
> "...shall stand possessed of the Trust Fund and the income thereof until the Vesting Day Upon Trust to..."
> 6. Twenty-one years represents the maximum fixed period for the accumulation of income.
> 7. Clause 4(1) gives the Trustees the option of returning the shares which represent accumulated profits to the existing shareholders. Although the shares are held on discretionary trusts the trust will be exempt from the periodic and exit charges normally levied on such trusts - ITA 1984 S.58(1)(b). There will be a charge to the Inheritance Tax upon the value of the fund at the end of the trust period — ITA 1984 S.72(2)(a). The charge is calculated according to a sliding scale of rates for each ten year period up to a maximum of 30% if the trust qualified under section 86 for fifty years or more. This charge,

(2) Provided that if there be no persons who qualify as Employees at that time and the Company shall have previously been put into liquidation to the persons who were Employees at the date of execution hereof in such shares as the Trustees shall appoint [and in default thereof in equal shares absolutely].[8]

5. Subject to and in default of the foregoing trusts and powers the Trust Fund shall be held Upon Trust for such one or more bodies which are established for purposes which are exclusively charitable according to the law of England and Wales as the Trustees or in default thereof Her Majesty's Attorney General shall determine.

6. (1) The Trustees shall have power to invest or lay out the whole or any part of the Trust Fund in the purchase of or at interest upon the security of such stocks funds shares securities or other investments or property (real or personal) of whatsoever nature and wheresoever situate and whether involving liability or not and whether producing income or not as the Trustees shall in their absolute discretion think fit to the intent that subject as aforesaid the Trustees shall have the same full and unrestricted powers of investing and transposing investments and laying out monies in all respects as if they were absolutely entitled thereto beneficially.

(2) Provided that the Trustees shall be at liberty to invest the Trust Fund in the shares of the Company after taking such valuations and upon such terms as to price and other conditions of payment as they shall think fit provided that without prejudice to the generality of the foregoing the Trustees shall have power to purchase the said shares at a price in excess of or less than their then market value[9] and in making such investments shall not be obliged to have regard to the need to diversify the investments of

however, may be avoided to the extent that the fund is appointed to charity — ITA 1984 S.76.
8. After the trust has been in existence for a long time it may be difficult to trace those persons (or those entitled under their will or intestacy) who were Employees at the time the Trust was set up. Clearly the Trustees have power to appoint the capital exclusively amongst those Employees they can locate. Where, however, the trust period is likely to be long and there is some chance that the Trustees will fail to exercise their power of appointment, it may be advisable to remove the provision in square brackets. In such event the list of names in Schedule II would no longer be necessary and in default of any appointment the Trust Fund would be held on the charitable trusts set out in Clause 5. A further alternative would be to remove the whole of sub-clause (2).
9. As presently drafted the Trustees have a very wide discretion to invest in the Company's shares whether at an undervalue or an overvalue. In certain cases, however, the members may wish to provide for an agreed method of valuation.

the Trust Fund but shall have regard to the need to secure the future of the Company and the contentment of the Employees.
(3) The Trustees shall have power to change or vary any investments for the time being forming part of the Trust Fund.
(4) The Trustees shall have power to permit any Beneficiary or Beneficiaries under the Trusts hereof to reside in any dwelling house or occupy or have the use of any land which is or the proceeds of sale of which may for the time being be subject to the trusts hereof upon such terms and conditions as the Trustees shall think fit.
(5) The Trustees shall have power to lend any part of the Trust Fund to Employees at such rate of interest or free of interest as the Trustees shall in their sole discretion determine for the purpose of enabling Employees to acquire shares in the Company
(6) The Trustees shall have power to borrow money on such terms and conditions as to interest repayment and otherwise as they may think fit and whether upon security of the whole or any part of the Trust Fund or upon their personal security only and to use the money so borrowed in making any investments hereby authorised.

7. Notwithstanding anything hereinbefore contained no part of the Trust Fund or the income thereof may be applied at any time for the benefit of any Beneficiary who is or has been an Excluded Person but so that this Clause shall not affect any power herein contained to make a payment which is the income of any person for any of the purposes of income tax or would be the income for any of those purposes of a person not resident in the United Kingdom if he were so resident.[10]

8. The power of appointing new Trustees shall be vested in the Company.

9. (1) Any Trustee being a solicitor, accountant or other person engaged in any profession or business shall be entitled to be paid all usual professional or proper charges for business transacted time expended or acts done by him or any partner of his in connection with the trusts hereof including acts which a Trustee

---

10. In order to qualify as an employee trust, the trust instrument must not permit capital to be applied for the benefit of certain participators in the company and other persons connected with them. However, shareholders who hold or are entitled to acquire less than five per cent of the equity are permitted to receive capital payments. Shareholders with five per cent or more may still receive payments from the trust which are taxed as income in their hands — see ITA 1984 S.28. See Note 4.

not being in any profession or business could have done personally.

(2) In the professed execution of the trusts and powers hereof no Trustee shall be liable for any loss of the Trust Fund arising by reason of any improper investment made in good faith or the negligence or fraud of any agent employed by him or by any other trustee hereof although the employment of such agent was not strictly necessary or expedient or by reason of any mistakes or omissions made in good faith by any Trustee hereof or by reason of any other matter or thing except wilful and individual fraud or wrongdoing on the part of the Trustee who is sought to be made so liable.

IN WITNESS etc

SCHEDULE 1

[Here set out the particulars of the Shares]

SCHEDULE 2

[Here set out a complete list of Employees at the time of the execution of this Deed]

To be executed by all parties

MODEL FORMS OR PRECEDENTS

SETTLEMENT II

Employee Trust Settlement as a Vehicle for a Gift of a Conventional Company to its Employees with Tax Relief

(see text, p.63)

THIS SETTLEMENT is made the   day of   19   BETWEEN AB OF [address] (hereinafter called "the Settlor") of the one part and CD of [address] and EF of [address] (hereinafter called "the Original Trustees") of the other part.

W H E R E A S :-

(A) The Settlor is beneficially entitled to the Ordinary Shares as are more particularly set out in Schedule I hereto (hereinafter called "the Shares") in the company YZ Limited whose registered office is at [address] (hereinafter called "the Company")[1]

(B) The Company carries on the business of [descripton of the Company's business];

(C) The Settlor wishes to encourage the staff of the Company by instituting the trusts contained in this Deed with the object of

---

1. The Recitals have been drafted to deal with a gift of existing shares by a major shareholder. The consequent transfer of value would be an exempt transfer — ITA 1984 S.28. However, with minor amendments, the draft would be a suitable vehicle for a settlement of cash by the company itself to finance the purchase of shares from existing shareholders. If the company is a "close company" the transfer of value made by the company would (in the absence of any relief) be apportioned amongst the individual participators in proportion to their holdings - ITA 1984 S.94. However the Precedent is intended also to satisfy the requirements of S.13 of the Inheritance Tax Act 1984 so that the company is deemed not to have made a transfer of value.
   The capital gains treatment of assets disposed of by the Company or the individual Settlor is the same. If the disposal is by way of gift or for actual consideration no greater than the disponor's base cost, in return for the trustees taking over the disponor's base cost, no chargeable gain will accrue to the disponor — CGTA 1979 S.149. However, it should be noted that the relief only applies to transactions between the trustees and individual shareholders where the transfer of value is exempt.

causing the shares to be held by the trustees hereof for the benefit of the staff their spouses relations and dependants

(D) The Settlor has transferred into the joint names of the Original Trustees the shares to be held upon the trustes hereof

(E) The Original Trustees now hold more than one half of the Ordinary Shares in the Company and have power to cast the majority of votes on all questions affecting the Company as a whole[2]

NOW THIS DEED WITNESSETH as follows:

1. In this Deed unless the context otherwise requires the following terms shall have the following meanings:

(1) "The Trustees" means the original trustees and other the trustees or trustee for the time being hereof.
(2) "Employee" means any person who at any time before the Vesting Day is employed by the Company under a contract of employment or holds office with the Comapny.[3]
(3) "Beneficiary" means any Employee[3] any spouse of any Employee any child or remoter issue (including for the avoidance of doubt any adopted child) of any employee and any person who in the opinion of the Trustees is a dependant of any Employee and Beneficiaries shall be construed accordingly.[4]
(4) "The Trust Fund" means:
 (i) The Shares;
 (ii) All property accepted by the Trustees as additions to the Trust Fund;
 (iii) All monies investments and property from time to time

---

2. S.28 imposes the additional condition that the trustees should, within one year of the transfer, have voting control over the affairs of the company — ITA S.28(2). Recital (E) will not be necessary in the case of a settlement by the company.
3. As presently drafted, a person who ceases to be employed by or to hold office with the company, will cease, along with his family, to be a beneficiary. Such a restricted class may coincide with certain people's views that the benefits from employee trusts should be strictly limited to the employees and their families during the period of their active involvement. However, the class of beneficiary may be extended to include former employees without losing tax privileges. If this is desired, a similar definition of Beneficiary to that in Clause 1(3) of Precedent I should be adopted.
4. If it is desired to make charities primary beneficiaries see note 2 to Settlement I and text p.70.

representing such shares and additions and any accumulations of income thereof.

(5) "The Vesting Day" means the day on which shall expire the period of [   ]⁵ from the date of the execution of this Deed (which period shall be the perpetuity period applicable hereto).
(6) "Excluded Person" means any person falling within Section 28(4) (and not within Section 28(5)) of the Inheritance Tax Act 1984 as amended and in force at the date of the execution of this Deed.⁶
(7) "Employees Organisation" means any body or association of persons whether incorporated or otherwise the membership of which is made up exclusively of all or most of the Employees which in the opinion of the Trustees satisfies the following conditions:

(i) any person upon ceasing to be an Employee shall cease to be a member of the said body or association;
(ii) the conduct and management of the affairs of the said body or association is subject to the supervision and control from time to time of the membership as a whole;
(iii) subject to (iv) and (v) below such supervision and control is exercised according to a majority of the members then voting and each member has equal voting rights on all questions affecting the body or association as a whole;
(iv) notwithstanding any requirement in (iii) above the rules of the said body or assocation may provide that certain questions may only be determined in accordance with a majority in excess of a simple majority of the members then voting;
(v) without prejudice to the generality of the foregoing the said rules shall provide that the body or association shall not be dissolved or wound up nor shall any voting rights in the Company under the control of the body or association be cast in favour of a special resolution of the Company, save upon the passing of a resolution by a majority of three fourths of the members who, being entitled to vote, vote in person at a meeting open to all members of which not less than [   ] days' notice, specifying the intention to propose a resolution to dissolve or wind up the body or association, or to exercise

---

5. See note 3 to Settlement I and text p.
6. In order to qualify as an employee trust, the trust instrument must not permit capital to be applied for the benefit of certain participators in the company and other persons connected with them. However, shareholders who hold or are entitled to acquire less than 5% of the equity are permitted to receive capital payments. Shareholders with 5% or more may still receive payments from the trust which are taxed as income in their hands — see ITA 1984 S.28. See Note 7.

such voting rights in the Company in favour of a special resolution of the Company, has been duly given;
(vi) further the said rules shall provide that the provisions in (v) above shall not be altered save upon passing of a resolution by a like majority of the members and in accordance with the similar procedures as those specified in that paragraph;
(vii) subject to (iv), (v) and (vi) above the said body or association on passing of the appropriate resolution may be wound up or otherwise dissolved and its assets divided amongst the members.

2. The Trustees shall stand possessed of the Trust Fund and the income thereof upon such trusts for the benefit of all or any one or more of the Beneficiaries exclusive of the other or others in such shares and proportions and subject to such terms and limitations as the Trustees before the Vesting Day but without infringing the rules against perpetuities shall in their absolute discretion appoint.[7]

3. (1) In default of and subject to any such appointment as aforesaid the Trustees shall:
(i) pay or apply the income of the Trust Fund within 12 months of its coming into their possession to or for the benefit of all or such one or more exclusive of the other or others of the Beneficiaries as shall then be living [or in existence] in such shares as the Trustees in their absolute discretion shall think fit and subject thereto to such of the Beneficiaries who are or have been Employees as shall then be living in equal shares absolutely;
(ii) provided always that during the period of 21 years from the date hereof[8] the Trustees shall have power to accumulate the whole or any part of the income by capitalising it as an accretion to and part of the Trust Fund;
(iii) stand possessed of the Trust Fund Upon Trust for all or such one or more of the Beneficiaries as shall then be living [or

---

7. The Trustees have power to distribute the whole or part of the capital at any time before the end of the trust period. For more limited alternatives to this power of appointment — see note 4 to Settlement I. Although the shares are held on discretionary trusts the trust will be exempt from the periodic and exit charges normally levied on such trusts - ITA 1984 S.58(1)(b). There will be a charge to Inheritance Tax upon the value of the fund at the end of the trust period - ITA 1984 S.72(2)(a). The charge is calculated according to a sliding scale of rates for each ten year period up to a maximum of 30% if the trust qualified under section 86 for fifty years or more. This charge, however, may be avoided to the extent that the fund is appointed to charity — ITA 1984 S.76.
8. See note 6 to Settlement I.

in existence] as the Trustees shall prior to or upon the Vesting Day determine and in default of such determination upon trust for such of the Beneficiaries who are or have been employees as shall then be living in equal shares absolutely.

4. Notwithstanding the foregoing trusts the Trustees shall have power on or before the Vesting Day to transfer absolutely the whole or any part of the Trust Fund to such Employees Organisations as they in their absolute discretion shall determine. In the event that the said Employees Organisation does not have separate legal personality any such transfer shall only take effect as an absolute beneficial gift to the then members of the said Employees Organisation as an accretion to its funds and subject only to the rules thereof.

5. Subject to and in default of the foregoing trusts and powers the Trust Fund shall be held Upon Trust for such one or more bodies of persons established for purposes which are exclusively charitable according to the law of England and Wales for the time being as the Trustees or in default thereof Her Majesty's Attorney General shall select.

6. (1) Any Trustee (other than the Settlor or any spouse of the Settlor) being a solicitor accountant or other person engaged in any profession or business shall be entitled to be paid all usual professional or proper charges for business transacted time expended and acts done by him or any partner of his in connection with the trusts hereof including acts which a Trustee not being in any profession or business could have done personally.
(2) In the professed execution of the trusts and powers hereof no Trustee shall be liable for any loss to the Trust Fund arising by reason of any improper investment made in good faith or the negligence or fraud of any agent employed by him or by any other Trustee hereof although the employment of such agent was not strictly necessary or expedient or by reason of any mistakes or omissions made in good faith by any Trustee hereof or by reason of any other matter or thing except wilful and individual fraud or wrongdoing on the part of the Trustee who is sought to be made so liable.

7. The power of appointing new Trustees shall during his lifetime be vested in the Settlor.

8. The powers and other provisions contained in Schedule 2

hereto shall until the Vesting Day and for such other period if any as the law shall allow apply so far as concerns the administration of the trusts hereof.

9. Notwithstanding anything contained in this Deed or in the Schedules hereto no part of the Trust Fund or the income thereof may be applied at any time for the benefit of any Beneficiary who is or has been an Excluded Person but so that this clause shall not affect any power herein contained to make a payment which is the income of any person for any of the purposes of income tax or would be the income for any of those purposes of a person not resident in the United Kingdom if he were so resident.[6]

10. Any reference in this Settlement to any enactment shall for the purpose of enabling the terms of this Settlement to comply with the conditions contained in Section 28 of the Inheritance Tax Act 1984 or Section 86 of the Inheritance Tax Act 1984 be construed as a reference to any modification, amendment or re-enactment thereof.

IN WITNESS etc

SCHEDULE 1

[Here set out details of the shares transferred into the Settlement]

SCHEDULE 2

The following powers and provisions shall until the Vesting Day and for such further period if any as the law shall allow apply so far as concerns the administration of the Trusts hereof:

The Trustees shall have the following powers:

(a) power to allow the property or investments for the time being subject to the trusts hereof to remain unsold or in the actual state of investment thereof so long as the Trustees shall think fit and at any time or times to sell call in or convert into money the said property or investments or any part or parts thereof;

(b) power to invest or lay out in the purchase of or at interest upon the security of such stocks funds shares securities or other investments or property (real or personal) of whatsoever nature and wheresoever situate and whether involving liability or not and whether producing income or not as the Trustees shall in their absolute discretion think fit to the intent that subject as aforesaid the Trustees shall have the same full and unrestricted powers of investing and transposing investments and laying out monies in all respects as if they were absolutely entitled thereto beneficially PROVIDED ALWAYS that the Trustees shall be at liberty to invest the Trust Fund in the shares of the Company and in making such investments shall not be obliged to have regard to the need to diversify the investments of the Trust Fund but shall have regard to the need to secure the future of the Company and the contentment of Employees;[9]

(c) power to exercise the widest possible managerial discretion permitted by law in the exercise of any voting rights or any other right attaching to any class or classes of shares in the Company from time to time subject to the trusts hereof to the intent that the Trustees shall have the same unfettered power of decision as if they were absolutely entitled thereto beneficially;[10]

(d) power to permit any Beneficiary or Beneficiaries under the Trusts hereof to reside in any dwelling house or occupy or have the use of any land which is or the proceeds of sale of which may for the time being be subject to the trusts hereof upon such terms and conditions as the Trustees shall decide;

(e) power to appropriate any investment or property from time to time forming part of the Trust Fund in its actual state of investment in or towards the satisfaction of the beneficial

---

9. See Clause 6(2) of Settlement I for a wider version of this power.
10. The Trustees are given a very wide discretion over the exercise of their share rights. Along with the power to appropriate in paragraph (e), the Trustees would be able to convert the Company into a worker controlled company and allocate the shares in the re-organised company *in specie* to the then employees — *see* p.69 of the text.

interest of any person in the Trust Fund upon making such valuation as the Trustees may think fit and without the necessity of obtaining the consent of any person;

(f) power to borrow money on such terms as to interest repayment and otherwise as they may think fit and whether upon the security of the whole or any part of the Trust Fund or upon their personal security only and to use money so borrowed in making any investments hereby authorised;

(g) power to lend any part of the Trust Fund to any Employee at such rate of interest or free of interest as the Trustees shall in their sole discretion determine for the purpose of enabling such Employee to acquire shares in the Company;

(h) power to consult with and seek advice from any Employee or Employees Employee Organisation or Organisations or any other body or association established to promote the interests of the Employees and in writing to delegate to any Employees Organisation or Organisations for one or more periods each not exceeding [months/years] the performance and exercise of such one or more of their powers duties and discretions as they in their absolute discretion shall think fit.[11]

(i) power in the case of any Trustee (other than the Settlor or any spouse of the Settlor) to retain without being liable to account therefor any reasonable remuneration from the office of director in any company whose shares formed part of the Trust Fund notwithstanding that the votes attaching to such shares may have enabled such Trustee to qualify or be elected as a director.

SCHEDULE 3

[Here set out a complete list of Employees at the time of the execution of the Deed.]

To be executed by all parties

---

11. The Trustees may transfer the performance of their duties and powers for limited periods of time to one or more suitable Employees Organisation without incurring liability for the subsequent conduct of the trust's affairs. If the employees organisation behaves responsibly, the Trustees may extend the period of delegation.

Appendix

Table A

(Published by HM Stationery Office in S.1. 1985 No. 805 as amended by S.1. 1985 No. 1052)

Regulations for Management of a Company Limited by Shares

INTERPRETATION

1. In these regulations —
"the Act" means the Companies Act 1985 including any statutory modification or re-enactment thereof for the time being in force.
"the articles" means the articles of the company.
"clear days" in relation to the period of a notice means that period excluding the day when the notice is given or deemed to be given and the day for which it is given or on which it is to take effect.
"executed" includes any mode of execution.
"office" means the registered office of the company.
"the holder" in relation to shares means the member whose name is entered in the register of members as the holder of the shares.
"the seal" means the common seal of the company.
"secretary" means the secretary of the company or any other person appointed to perform the duties of the secretary of the company, including a joint, assistant or deputy secretary.
"the United Kingdom" means Great Britain and Northern Ireland.

Unless the context otherwise requires, words or expressions contained in these regulations bear the same meaning as in the Act but excluding any statutory modification thereof not in force when these regulations become binding on the company.

SHARE CAPITAL

2. Subject to the provisions of the Act and without prejudice to any rights attached to any existing shares, any share may be issued with such rights or restrictions as the company may by ordinary resolution determine.

3. Subject to the provisions of the Act, shares may be issued which are to be redeemed or are to be liable to be redeemed at the option of the company or the holder on such terms and in such manner as may be provided by the articles.

4. The company may exercise the powers of paying commissions conferred by the Act. Subject to the provisions of the Act, any such commission may be satisfied by the payment of cash or by the allotment of fully or partly paid shares or partly in one way and partly in the other.

5. Except as required by law, no person shall be recognised by the company as holding any share upon any trust and (except as otherwise provided by the articles or by law) the company shall not be bound by or recognise any interest in any share except an absolute right to the entirety thereof in the holder.

SHARE CERTIFICATES

6. Every member, upon becoming the holder of any shares, shall be entitled without payment to one certificate for all the shares of each class held by him (and, upon transferring a part of his holding of shares of any class, to a certificate for the balance of such holding) or several certificates each for one or more of his shares upon payment for every certificate after the first of such reasonable sum as the directors may determine. Every certificate shall be sealed with the seal and shall specify the number, class and distinguishing numbers (if any) of the shares to which it relates and the amount or respective amounts paid up thereon. The company shall not be bound to issue more than one certificate for shares held jointly by several persons and delivery of a certificate to one joint holder shall be a sufficient delivery to all of them.

7. If a share certificate is defaced, worn-out, lost or destroyed, it may be renewed on such terms (if any) as to evidence and indemnity and payment of the expenses reasonably incurred by the company in investigating evidence as the directors may determine but otherwise free of charge, and (in the case of defacement or wearing-out) on delivery up of the old certificate.

LIEN

(Excluded by Article 1.)

8. The company shall have a first and paramount lien on every share (not being a fully paid share) for all moneys (whether presently payable or not) payable at a fixed time or called in

respect of that share. The directors may at any time declare any share to be wholly or in part exempt from the provisions of this regulation. The company's lien on a share shall extend to any amount payable in respect of it.

9. The company may sell in such manner as the directors determine any shares on which the company has a lien if a sum in respect of which the lien exists is presently payable and is not paid within fourteen clear days after notice has been given to the holder of the share or to the person entitled to it in consequence of the death or bankruptcy of the holder, demanding payment and stating that if the notice is not complied with the shares may be sold.

10. To give effect to a sale the directors may authorise some person to execute an instrument of transfer of the shares sold to, or in accordance with the directions of, the purchaser. The title of the transferee to the shares shall not be affected by any irregularity in or invalidity of the proceedings in reference to the sale.

11. The net proceeds of the sale, after payment of the costs, shall be applied in payment of so much of the sum for which the lien exists as is presently payable, and any residue shall (upon surrender to the company for cancellation of the certificate for the shares sold and subject to a like lien for any moneys not presently payable as existed upon the shares before the sale) be paid to the person entitled to the shares at the date of the sale.

CALLS ON SHARES AND FORFEITURE

12. Subject to the terms of allotment, the directors may make calls upon the members in respect of any moneys unpaid on their shares (whether in respect of nominal value or premium) and each member shall (subject to receiving at least fourteen clear days' notice specifying when and where payment is to be made) pay to the company as required by the notice the amount called on his shares. A call may be required to be paid by instalments. A call may, before receipt by the company of any sum due thereunder, be revoked in whole or part and payment of a call may be postponed in whole or part. A person upon whom a call is made shall remain liable for calls made upon him notwithstanding the subsequent transfer of the shares in respect whereof the call was made.

13. A call shall be deemed to have been made at the time when the resolution of the directors authorising the call was passed.

14. The joint holders of a share shall be jointly and severally liable to pay all calls in respect thereof.

15. If a call remains unpaid after it has become due and payable the person from whom it is due and payable shall pay interest on the amount unpaid from the day it became due and payable until it is paid at the rate fixed by the terms of allotment of the share or in the notice of the call or, if no rate is fixed, at the appropriate rate (as defined by the Act) but the directors may waive payment of the interest wholly or in part.

16. An amount payable in respect of a share on allotment or at any fixed date, whether in respect of nominal value or premium or as an instalment of a call, shall be deemed to be a call and if it is not paid the provisions of the articles shall apply as if that amount had become due and payable by virtue of a call.

17. Subject to the terms of allotment, the directors may make arrangements on the issue of shares for a difference between the holders in the amounts and times of payment of calls on their shares.

18. If a call remains unpaid after it has become due and payable the directors may give to the person from whom it is due not less than fourteen clear days' notice requiring payment of the amount unpaid together with any interest which may have accrued. The notice shall name the place where payment is to be made and shall state that if the notice is not complied with the shares in respect of which the call was made will be liable to be forfeited.

19. If the notice is not complied with any share in respect of which it was given may, before the payment required by the notice has been made, be forfeited by a resolution of the directors and the forfeiture shall include all dividends or other moneys payable in respect of the forfeited shares and not paid before the forfeiture.

20. Subject to the provisions of the Act, a forfeited share may be sold, re-allotted or otherwise disposed of on such terms and in such manner as the directors determine either to the person who was before the forfeiture the holder or to any other person and at any time before sale, re-allotment or other disposition, the forfeiture may be cancelled on such terms as the directors think

fit. Where for the purposes of its disposal a forfeited share is to be transferred to any person the directors may authorise some person to execute an instrument of transfer of the share to that person.

21. A person any of whose shares have been forfeited shall cease to be a member in respect of them and shall surrender to the company for cancellation the certificate for the shares forfeited but shall remain liable to the company for all moneys which at the date of forfeiture were presently payable by him to the company in respect of those shares with interest at the rate at which interest was payable on those moneys before the forfeiture or, if no interest was so payable, at the appropriate rate (as defined in the Act) from the date of forfeiture until payment but the directors may waive payment wholly or in part or enforce payment without any allowance for the value of the shares at the time of forfeiture or for any consideration received on their disposal.

22. A statutory declaration by a director or the secretary that a share has been forfeited on a specified date shall be conclusive evidence of the facts stated in it as against all persons claiming to be entitled to the share and the declaration shall (subject to the execution of an instrument of transfer if necessary) constitute a good title to the share and the person to whom the share is disposed of shall not be bound to see to the application of the consideration, if any, nor shall his title to the share be affected by any irregularity in or invalidity of the proceedings in reference to the forfeiture or disposal of the share.

TRANSFER OF SHARES

23. The instrument of transfer of a share may be in any usual form or in any other form which the directors may approve and shall be executed by or on behalf of the transferor and, unless the share is fully paid, by or on behalf of the transferee.

24. The directors may refuse to register the transfer of a share which is not fully paid to a person of whom they do not approve and they may refuse to register the transfer of a share on which the company has a lien. They may also refuse to register a tranfer unless —

  (a) it is lodged at the office or at such other place as the directors may appoint and is accompanied by the certificate for the shares to which it relates and such other

evidence as the directors may reasonably require to show the right of the transferor to make the transfer;
(b) it is in respect of only one class of shares; and
(c) it is in favour of not more than four transferees.

25. If the directors refuse to register a transfer of a share, they shall within two months after the date on which the transfer was lodged with the company send to the transferee notice of the refusal.

26. The registration of transfers of shares or of transfers of any class of shares may be suspended at such times and for such periods (not exceeding thirty days in any year) as the directors may determine.

27. No fee shall be charged for the registration of any instrument of transfer or other document relating to or affecting the title to any share.

28. The company shall be entitled to retain any instrument of transfer which is registered, but any instrument of transfer which the directors refuse to register shall be returned to the person lodging it when notice of the refusal is given.

TRANSMISSION OF SHARES

29. If a member dies the survivor or survivors where he was a joint holder, and his personal representatives where he was a sole holder or the only survivor of joint holders, shall be the only persons recognised by the company as having any title to his interest; but nothing herein contained shall release the estate of a deceased member from any liability in respect of any share which had been jointly held by him.

30. A person becoming entitled to a share in consequence of the death or bankruptcy of a member may, upon such evidence being produced as the directors may properly require, elect either to become the holder of the share or to have some person nominated by him registered as the transferee. If he elects to become the holder he shall give notice to the company to that effect. If he elects to have another person registered he shall execute an instrument of transfer of the share to that person. All the articles relating to the transfer of shares shall apply to the notice or instrument of transfer as if it were an instrument of

transfer executed by the member and the death or bankruptcy of the member had not occurred.

31. A person becoming entitled to a share in consequence of the death or bankruptcy of a member shall have the rights to which he would be entitled if he were the holder of the share, except that he shall not, before being registered as the holder of the share, be entitled in respect of it to attend or vote at any meeting of the company or at any separate meeting of the holders of any class of shares in the company.

ALTERATION OF SHARE CAPITAL

32. The company may by ordinary resolution —
    (a) increase its share capital by new shares of such amount as the resolution prescribes;
    (b) consolidate and divide all or any of its share capital into shares of larger amount than its existing shares;
    (c) subject to the provisions of the Act, sub-divide its shares, or any of them, into shares of smaller amount and the resolution may determine that, as between the shares resulting from the sub-division, any of them may have any preference or advantage as compared with the others; and
    (d) cancel shares which, at the date of the passing of the resolution, have not been taken or agreed to be taken by any person and diminish the amount of its share capital by the amount of the shares so cancelled.

33. Whenever as a result of a consolidation of shares any members would become entitled to fractions of a share, the directors may, on behalf of those members, sell the shares representing the fractions for the best price reasonably obtainable to any person (including, subject to the provisions of the Act, the company) and distribute the net proceeds of sale in due proportion among those members, and the directors may authorise some person to execute an instrument of transfer of the shares to, or in accordance with the directions of, the purchaser. The transferee shall not be bound to see to the application of the purchase money nor shall his title to the shares be affected by any irregularity in or invalidity of the proceedings in reference to the sale.

34. Subject to the provisions of the Act, the company may by special resolution reduce its share capital, any capital redemption reserve and any share premium account in any way.

PURCHASE OF OWN SHARES

35. Subject to the provisions of the Act, the company may purchase its own shares (including any redeemable shares) and, it it is a private company, make a payment in respect of the redemption or purchase of its own shares otherwise than out of distributable profits of the company or the proceeds of a fresh issue of shares.

GENERAL MEETINGS

36. All general meetings other than annual general meetings shall be called extraordinary general meetings.

(Excluded by Article 1.) 37. The directors may call general meetings and, on the requisition of members pursuant to the provisions of the Act, shall forthwith proceed to convene an extraordinary general meeting for a date not later than eight weeks after receipt of the requisition. If there are not within the United Kingdom sufficient directors to call a general meeting, any director or any member of the company may call a general meeting.

NOTICE OF GENERAL MEETINGS

38. An annual general meeting and an extraordinary general meeting called for the passing of a special resolution or a resolution appointing a person as a director shall be called by at least twenty-one clear days' notice. All other extraordinary general meetings shall be called by at least fourteen clear days' notice but a general meeting may be called by shorter notice if it is so agreed —
    (a) in the case of an annual general meeting, by all the members entitled to attend and vote thereat; and
    (b) in the case of any other meeting by a majority in number of the members having a right to attend and vote being a majority together holding not less than ninety-five per cent. in nominal value of the shares giving that right.

The notice shall specify the time and place of the meeting and the general nature of the business to be transacted and, in the case of an annual general meeting, shall specify the meeting as such.

Subject to the provisions of the articles and to any restrictions imposed on any shares, the notice shall be given to all the members, to all persons entitled to a share in consequence of the death or bankruptcy of a member and to the directors and auditors.

APPENDIX

39. The accidental ommission to give notice of a meeting to, or the non-receipt of notice of a meeting by, any person entitled to receive notice shall not invalidate the proceedings at that meeting.

PROCEEDINGS AT GENERAL MEETINGS

luded by cle 1.) 40. No business shall be transacted at any meeting unless a quorum is present. Two persons entitled to vote upon the business to be transacted, each being a member or a proxy for a member or a duly authorised representative of a corporation, shall be a quorum.

luded by cle 1.) 41. If such a quorum is not present within half an hour from the time appointed for the meeting, or if during a meeting such a quorum ceases to be present, the meeting shall stand adjoured to the same day in the next week at the same time and place or to such time and place as the directors may determine.

42. The chairman, if any, of the board of directors or in his absence some other director nominated by the directors shall preside as chairman of the meeting, but if neither the chairman nor such other director (if any) be present within fifteen minutes after the time appointed for holding the meeting and willing to act, the directors present shall elect one of their number to be chairman and, if there is only one director present and willing to act, he shall be chairman.

43. If no director is willing to act as chairman, or if no director is present within fifteen minutes after the time appointed for holding the meeting, the members present and entitled to vote shall choose one of their number to be chairman.

44. A director shall, notwithstanding that he is not a member, be entitled to attend and speak at any general meeting and at any separate meeting of the holders of any class of shares in the company.

45. The chairman may, with the consent of a meeting at which a quorum is present (and shall if so directed by the meeting), adjourn the meeting from time to time and from place to place, but no business shall be transacted at an adjourned meeting other than business which might properly have been transacted at the meeting had the adjournment not taken place. When a meeting is adjourned for fourteen days or more, at least seven clear days'

notice shall be given specifying the time and place of the adjourned meeting and the general nature of the business to be transacted. Otherwise it shall not be necessary to give any such notice.

(Excluded by Article 1.) 46. A resolution put to the vote of a meeting shall be decided on a show of hands unless before, or on the declaration of the result of, the show of hands a poll is duly demanded. Subject to the provisions of the Act, a poll may be demanded —
   (a) by the chairman, or
   (b) by at least two members having the right to vote at the meeting; or
   (c) by a member or members representing not less than one-tenth of the total voting rights of all the members having the right to vote at the meeting; or
   (d) by a member or members holding shares conferring a right to vote at the meeting being shares on which an aggregate sum has been paid up equal to not less than one-tenth of the total sum paid up on all the shares conferring that right;

and a demand by a person as proxy for a member shall be the same as a demand by the member.

47. Unless a poll is duly demanded a declaration by the chairman that a resolution has been carried or carried unanimously, or by a particular majority, or lost, or not carried by a particular majority and an entry to that effect in the minutes of the meeting shall be conclusive evidence of the fact without proof of the number or proportion of the votes recorded in favour of or against the resolution.

48. The demand for a poll may, before the poll is taken, be withdrawn but only with the consent of the chairman and a demand so withdrawn shall not be taken to have invalidated the result of a show of hands declared before the demand was made.

49. A poll shall be taken as the chairman directs and he may appoint scrutineers (who need not be members) and fix a time and place for declaring the result of the poll. The result of the poll shall be deemed to be the resolution of the meeting at which the poll was demanded.

50. In the case of an equality of votes, whether on a show of

hands or on a poll, the chairman shall be entitled to a casting vote in addition to any other vote he may have.

51. A poll demanded on the election of a chairman or on a question of adjournment shall be taken forthwith. A poll demanded on any other question shall be taken either forthwith or at such time and place as the chairman directs not being more than thirty days after the poll is demanded. The demand for a poll shall not prevent the continuance of a meeting for the transaction of any business other than the question on which the poll was demanded. If a poll is demanded before the declaration of the result of a show of hands and the demand is duly withdrawn, the meeting shall continue as if the demand had not been made.

52. No notice need be given of a poll not taken forthwith if the time and place at which it is to be taken are announced at the meeting at which it is demanded. In any other case at least seven clear days' notice shall be given specifying the time and place at which the poll is to be taken.

53. A resolution in writing executed by or on behalf of each member who would have been entitled to vote upon if if it had been proposed at a general meeting at which he was present shall be as effectual as if it had been passed at a general meeting duly convened and held and may consist of several instruments in the like form each executed by or on behalf of one or more members.

VOTES OF MEMBERS

(xcluded by rticle 1.)

54. Subject to any rights or restrictions attached to any shares, on a show of hands every member who (being an individual) is present in person or (being a corporation) is present by a duly authorised representative, not being himself a member entitled to vote, shall have one vote and on a poll every member shall have one vote for every share of which he is the holder.

55. In the case of joint holders the vote of the senior who tenders a show of hands every member who (being any individual) is present in person or (being a corporation) is present by a duly authorised representative, not being himself a member entitled to vote, shall have one vote and on a poll every member shall have one vote for every share of which he is the holder.

56. A member in respect of whom an order has been made by any court having jurisdiction (whether in the United Kingdom or elsewhere) in matters concerning mental disorder may vote, whether on a show of hands or on a poll, by his receiver, curator

bonis or other person authorised in that behalf appointed by that court, and any such receiver, curator bonis or other person may, on a poll, vote by proxy. Evidence to the satisfaction of the directors of the authority of the person claiming to exercise the right to vote shall be deposited at the office, or at such other place as is specified in accordance with the articles for the deposit of instruments of proxy, not less than 48 hours before the time appointed for holding the meeting or adjourned meeting at which the right to vote is to be exercised and in default the right to vote shall not be exercisable.

57. No member shall vote at any general meeting or at any separate meeting of the holders of any class of shares in the company, either in person or by proxy, in respect of any share held by him unless all moneys presently payable by him in respect of that share have been paid.

58. No objection shall be raised to the qualification of any voter except at the meeting or adjourned meeting at which the vote objected to is tendered, and every vote not disallowed at the meeting shall be valid. Any objection made in due time shall be referred to the chairman whose decision shall be final and conclusive.

(Excluded by Article 1.) 59. On a poll votes may be given either personally or by proxy. A member may appoint more than one proxy to attend on the same occasion.

60. An instrument appointing a proxy shall be in writing, executed by or on behalf of the appointor and shall be in the following form (or in a form as near thereto as circumstances allow or in any other form which is usual or which the directors may approve) —

"   PLC/Limited
     I/We,   , of
                                           , being a
member/members of the above-named company, hereby appoint
                              of
                    , or failing him,
of   , as my/our proxy to vote in my/our name[s] and on my/our behalf at the annual/extraordinary general meeting of the company to be held on   19   , and at any adjournment thereof.
Signed on   19   ."

Appendix

61. Where it is desired to afford members an opportunity of instructing the proxy how he shall act the instrument appointing a proxy shall be in the following form (or in a form as near thereto as circumstances allow or in any other form which is usual or which the directors may approve) —

"   PLC/Limited
         I/We,   , of
                                                  , being a member/members of the above-named company, hereby appoint
                           of
                           , or failing him
of   , as my/our proxy to vote in my/our name[s] and on my/our behalf at the annual/extraordinary general meeting of the company to be held on   19   , and at any adjournment thereof.

This form is to be used in respect of the resolutions mentioned below as follows:

Resolution No. 1 *for *against
Resolution No. 2 *for *against.

*Strike out whichever is not desired.

Unless otherwise instructed, the proxy may vote as he thinks fit or abstain from voting.

Signed this   day of   19   ."

(modified by article 20.) 62. The instrument appointing a proxy and any authority under which it is executed or a copy of such authority certified notarially or in some other way approved by the directors may —
  (a) be deposited at the office or at such other place within the United Kingdom as is specified in the notice convening the meeting or in any instrument of proxy sent out by the company in relation to the meeting not less than 48 hours before the time for holding the meeting or adjourned meeting at which the person named in the instrument proposes to vote; or
  (b) in the case of a poll taken more than 48 hours after it is demanded, be deposited as aforesaid after the poll has been demanded and not less than 24 hours before the time appointed for the taking of the poll; or
  (c) where the poll is not taken forthwith but is taken not more than 48 hours after it was demanded, be delivered at the

meeting at which the poll was demanded to the chairman or to the secretary or to any director;

and an instrument of proxy which is not deposited or delivered in a manner so permitted shall be invalid.

63. A vote given or poll demanded by proxy or by the duly authorised representative of a corporation shall be valid notwithstanding the previous determination of the authority of the person voting or demanding a poll unless notice of the determination was received by the company at the office or at such other place at which the instrument of proxy was duly deposited before the commencement of the meeting or adjourned meeting at which the vote is given or the poll demanded or (in the case of a poll taken otherwise than on the same day as the meeting or adjourned meeting) the time appointed for taking the poll.

NUMBER OF DIRECTORS

64. Unless otherwise determined by ordinary resolution, the number of directors (other than alternate directors) shall not be subject to any maximum but shall be not less than two.

ALTERNATE DIRECTORS

65. Any director (other than an alternate director) may appoint any other director, or any other person approved by resolution of the directors and willing to act, to be an alternate director and may remove from office an alternate director so appointed by him.

66. An alternate director shall be entitled to receive notice of all meetings of directors and of all meetings of committees of directors of which his appointor is a member, to attend and vote at any such meeting at which the director appointing him is not personally present, and generally to perform all the functions of his appointor as a director in his absence but shall not be entitled to receive any remuneration from the company for his services as an alternate director. But it shall not be necessary to give notice of such a meeting to an alternate director who is absent from the United Kingdom.

67. An alternate director shall cease to be an alternate director if his appointor ceases to be a director; but, if a director retires by rotation or otherwise but is reappointed or deemed to have been

reappointed at the meeting at which he retires, any appointment of an alternate director made by him which was in force immediately prior to his retirement shall continue after his reappointment.

68. Any appointment or removal of an alternate director shall be by notice to the company signed by the director making or revoking the appointment or in any other manner approved by the directors.

69. Save as otherwise provided in the articles, an alternate director shall be deemed for all purposes to be a director and shall alone be responsible for his own acts and defaults and he shall not be deemed to be the agent of the director appointing him.

POWERS OF DIRECTORS

70. Subject to the provisions of the Act, the memorandum and the articles and to any directions given by special resolution, the business of the company shall be managed by the directors who may exercise all the powers of the company. No alteration of the memorandum or articles and no such direction shall invalidate any prior act of the directors which would have been valid if that alteration had not been made or that direction had not been given. The powers given by this regulation shall not be limited by any special power given to the directors by the articles and a meeting of directors at which a quorum is present may exercise all powers exercisable by the directors.

71. The directors may, by power of attorney or otherwise, appoint any person to be the agent of the company for such purposes and on such conditions as they determine, including authority for the agent to delegate all or any of his powers.

DELEGATION OF DIRECTORS' POWERS

72. The directors may delegate any of their powers to any committee consisting of one or more directors. They may also delegate to any managing director or any director holding any other executive office such of their powers as they consider desirable to be exercised by him. Any such delegation may be made subject to any conditions the directors may impose, and either collaterally with or to the exclusion of their own powers and may be revoked or altered. Subject to any such conditions, the proceedings of a committee with two or more members shall

be governed by the articles regulating the proceedings of directors so far as they are capable of applying.

APPOINTMENT AND RETIREMENT OF DIRECTORS

(Excluded by Article 1.) 73. At the first annual general meeting all the directors shall retire from office, and at every subsequent annual general meeting one-third of the directors who are subject to retirement by rotation or, if their number is not three or a multiple of three, the number nearest to one-third shall retire from office; but, if there is only one director who is subject to retirement by rotation, he shall retire.

(Excluded by Article 1.) 74. Subject to the provisions of the Act, the directors to retire by rotation shall be those who have been longest in office since their last appointment or reappointment, but as between persons who became or were last reappointed directors on the same day those to retire shall (unless they otherwise agree among themselves) be determined by lot.

(Excluded by Article 1.) 75. If the company, at the meeting at which a director retires by rotation, does not fill the vacancy the retiring director shall, if willing to act, he deemed to have been reappointed unless at the meeting it is resolved not to fill the vacancy or unless a resolution for the reappointment of the director is put to the meeting and lost.

(Excluded by Article 1.) 76. No person other than a director retiring by rotation shall be appointed or reappointed a director at any general meeting unless —
(a) he is recommended by the directors; or
(b) not less than fourteen nor more than thirty-five clear days before the date appointed for the meeting, notice executed by a member qualified to vote at the meeting has been given to the company of the intention to propose that person for appointment or reappointment stating the particulars which would, if he were so appointed or reappointed, be required to be included in the company's register of directors together with notice executed by that person of his willingness to be appointed or reappointed.

(Excluded by Article 1.) 77. Not less than seven nor more than twenty-eight clear days before the date appointed for holding a general meeting notice shall be given to all who are entitled to receive notice of the meeting of any person (other than a director retiring by rotation at the meeting) who is recommended by the directors for appointment or reappointment as a director at the meeting or in respect of whom notice has been duly given to the company of the intention to propose him at the meeting for appointment or reappointment as a director. The notice shall give the particulars of that person which would, if he were so appointed or reappointed, be required to be included in the company's register of directors.

(excluded by Article 1.) 78. Subject as aforesaid, the company may by ordinary resolution appoint a person who is willing to act to be a director either to fill a vacancy or as an additional director and may also determine the rotation in which any additional directors are to retire.

(excluded by Article 1.) 79. The directors may appoint a person who is willing to act to be a director, either to fill a vacancy or as an additional director, provided that the appointment does not cause the number of directors to exceed any number fixed by or in accordance with the articles as the maximum number of directors. A director so appointed shall hold office only until the next following annual general meeting and shall not be taken into account in determining the directors who are to retire by rotation at the meeting. If not reappointed at such annual general meeting, he shall vacate office at the conclusion thereof.

(excluded by Article 1.) 80. Subject as aforesaid, a director who retires at an annual general meeting may, if willing to act, be reappointed. If he is not reappointed, he shall retain office until the meeting appoints someone in his place, or if it does not do so, until the end of the meeting.

DISQUALIFICATION AND REMOVAL OF DIRECTORS

81. The office of a director shall be vacated if —
    (a) he ceases to be a director by virtue of any provision of the Act or he becomes prohibited by law from being a director; or
    (b) he becomes bankrupt or makes any arrangement or composition with his creditors generally; or
    (c) he is, or may be, suffering from mental disorder and either —
        (i) he is admitted to hospital in pursuance of an application for admission for treatment under the Mental Health Act 1983 or, in Scotland, an application for admission

under the Mental Health (Scotland) Act 1960, or
(ii) an order is made by a court having jurisdiction (whether in the United Kingdom or elsewhere) in matters concerning mental disorder for his detention or for the appointment of a receiver, curator bonis or other person to exercise powers with respect to his property or affairs; or
(d) he resigns his office by notice to the company; or
(e) he shall for more than six consecutive months have been absent without permission of the directors from meetings of directors held during that period and the directors resolve that his office be vacated.

(Modified by Article 23.) 82. The directors shall be entitled to such remuneration as the company may by ordinary resolution determine and, unless the resolution provides otherwise, the remuneration shall be deemed to accrue from day to day.

DIRECTORS' EXPENSES

83. The directors may be paid all travelling, hotel, and other expenses properly incurred by them in connection with their attendance at meetings of directors or committees of directors or general meetings or separate meetings of the holders of any class of shares or of debentures of the company or otherwise in connection with the discharge of their duties.

DIRECTORS' APPOINTMENTS AND INTERESTS

(Modified by Article 24.) 84. Subject to the provisions of the Act, the directors may appoint one or more of their number to the office of managing director or to any other executive office under the company and may enter into an agreement or arrangement with any director for his employment by the company or for the provision by him of any services outside the scope of the ordinary duties of a director. Any such appointment, agreement of arrangement may be made upon such terms as the directors determine and they may remunerate any such director for his services as they think fit. Any appointment of a director to an executive office shall terminate if he ceases to be a director but without prejudice to any claim to damages for breach of the contract of service between the director and the company. A managing director a director holding any other executive office shall not be subject to retirement by rotation.

85. Subject to the provisions of the Act, and provided that he has disclosed to the directors the nature and extent of any material interest of his, a director notwithstanding his office —
- (a) may be a party to, or otherwise interested in, any transaction or arrangement with the company or in which the company is otherwise interested;
- (b) may be a director or other officer of, or employed by, or a party to any transaction or arrangement with, or otherwise interested in, any body corporate promoted by the company or in which the company is otherwise interested; and
- (c) shall not, by reason of his office, be accountable to the company for any benefit which he derives from any such office or employment or from any such transaction or arrangement or from any interest in any such body corporate and no such transaction or arrangement shall be liable to be avoided on the ground of any such interest or benefit.

86. For the purposes of regulation 85 —
- (a) a general notice given to the directors that a director is to be regarded as having an interest of the nature and extent specified in the notice in any transaction or arrangement in which a specified person or class or persons is interested shall be deemed to be a disclosure that the director has an interest in any such transaction of the nature and extent so specified; and
- (b) an interest of which a director has no knowledge and of which it is unreasonable to expect him to have knowledge shall not be treated as an interest of his.

DIRECTORS' GRATUITIES AND PENSIONS

(Modified by Article 24.)

87. The directors may provide benefits, whether by the payment of gratuities or pensions or by insurance or otherwise, for any director who has held but no longer holds any executive office or employment with the company or with any body corporate which is or has been a subsidiary of the company or a predecessor in business of the company or of any such subsidiary, and for any member of his family (including a spouse and a former spouse) or any person who is or was dependent on him, and may (as well before as after he ceases to hold such office or employment) contribute to any fund and pay premiums for the purchase or provision of any such benefit.

PROCEEDINGS OF DIRECTORS

(Excluded by Article 1.) 88. Subject to the provisions of the articles, the directors may regulate their proceedings as they think fit. A director may, and the secretary at the request of a director shall, call a meeting of the directors. It shall not be necessary to give notice of a meeting to a director who is absent from the United Kingdom. Questions arising at a meeting shall be decided by a majority of votes. In the case of an equality of votes, the chairman shall have a second or casting vote. A director who is also an alternate director shall be entitled in the absence of his appointor to a separate vote on behalf of his appointor in addition to his own vote.

(Excluded by Article 1.) 89. The quorum for the transaction of the business of the directors may be fixed by the directors and unless so fixed at any other number shall be two. A person who holds office only as an alternate director shall, if his appointor is not present, be counted in the quorum.

90. The continuing directors or a sole continuing director may act notwithstanding any vacancies in their number, but, it the number of directors is less than the number fixed as the quorum, the continuing directors or director may act only for the purpose of filling vacancies or of calling a general meeting.

91. The directors may appoint one of their number to be the chairman of the board of directors and may at any time remove him from that office. Unless he is unwilling to do so, the director so appointed shall preside at every meeting of directors at which he is present. But if there is no director holding that office, or if the director holding it is unwilling to preside or is not present within five minutes after the time appointed for the meeting, the directors present may appoint one of their number to be chairman of the meeting.

92. All acts done by a meeting of directors, or of a committee of directors, or by a person acting as a director shall, notwithstanding that it be afterwards discovered that there was a defect in the appointment of any director or that any of them were disqualified from holding office, or had vacated office, or were not entitled to vote, be as valid as if every such person had been duly appointed and was qualified and had continued to be a director and had been entitled to vote.

93. A resolution in writing signed by all the directors entitled to receive notice of a meeting of directors or of a committee of

directors shall be as valid and effectual as if it had been passed at a meeting of directors or (as the case may be) a committee of directors duly convened and held and may consist of several documents in the like form each signed by one or more directors; but a resolution signed by an alternate director need not also be signed by his appointor and, if it is signed by a director who has appointed an alternate director, it need not be signed by the alternate director in that capacity.

94. Save as otherwise provided by the articles, a director shall not vote at a meeting of directors or of a committee of directors on any resolution concerning a matter in which he has, directly or indirectly, an interest or duty which is material and which conflicts or may conflict with the interests of the company unless his interest or duty arises only because the case falls within one or more of the following paragraphs —
  (a) the resolution relates to the giving to him of a guarantee, security, or indemnity in respect of money lent to, or an obligation incurred by him for the benefit of, the company or any of its subsidiaries;
  (b) the resolution relates to the giving to a third party of a guarantee, security, or indemnity in respect of an obligation of the company or any of its subsidiaries for which the director has assumed responsibility in whole or part and whether alone or jointly with others under a guarantee or indemnity or by the giving of security;
  (c) his interest arises by virtue of his subscribing or agreeing to subscribe for any shares, debentures or other securities of the company or any of its subsidiaries, or by virtue of his being, or intending to become, a participant in the underwriting or sub-underwriting of an offer of any such shares, debentures, or other securities by the company or any of its subsidiaries for subscription, purchase or exchange;
  (d) the resolution relates in any way to a retirement benefits scheme which has been approved, or is conditional upon approval, by the Board of Inland Revenue for taxation purposes.

For the purposes of this regulation, an interest of a person who is, for any purpose of the Act (excluding any statutory modification thereof not in force when this regulation becomes binding on the company), connected with a director shall be treated as an interest of the director and, in relation to an alternate director, an interest of his appointor shall be treated as an interest of the alternate director without prejudice to any interest which the alternate director has otherwise.

95. A director shall not be counted in the quorum present at a meeting in relation to a resolution on which he is not entitled to vote.

96. The company may by ordinary resolution suspend or relax to any extent, either generally or in respect of any particular matter, any provision of the articles prohibiting a director from voting at a meeting of directors or of a committee of directors.

97. Where proposals are under consideration concerning the appointment of two or more directors to offices or employments with the company or any body corporate in which the company is interested the proposals may be divided and considered in relation to each director separately and (provided he is not for another reason precluded from voting) each of the directors concerned shall be entitled to vote and be counted in the quorum in respect of each resolution except that concerning his own appointment.

98. If a question arises at a meeting of directors or of a committee of directors as to the right of a director to vote, the question may, before the conclusion of the meeting, be referred to the chairman of the meeting and his ruling in relation to any director other than himself shall be final and conclusive.

SECRETARY

(Modified by Article 24.) 99. Subject to the provisions of the Act, the secretary shall be appointed by the directors for such term, at such remuneration and upon such conditions as they may think fit; and any secretary so appointed may be removed by them.

MINUTES

100. The directors shall cause minutes to be made in books kept for the purpose —
    (a) of all appointments of officers made by the directors; and
    (b) of all proceedings at meetings of the company, of the holders of any class of shares in the company, and of the directors, and of committees of directors, including the names of the directors present at each such meeting.

APPENDIX

THE SEAL

101. The seal shall only be used by the authority of the directors or of a committee of directors authorised by the directors. The directors may determine who shall sign any instrument to which the seal is affixed and unless otherwise so determined it shall be signed by a director and by the secretary or by a second director.

DIVIDENDS

102. Subject to the provisions of the Act, the company may by ordinary resolution declare dividends in accordance with the respective rights of the members, but no dividend shall exceed the amount recommended by the directors.

103. Subject to the provisions of the Act, the directors may pay interim dividends if it appears to them that they are justified by the profits of the company available for distribution. If the share capital is divided into different classes, the directors may pay interim dividends on shares which confer deferred or non-preferred rights with regard to dividend as well as on shares which confer preferential rights with regard to dividend, but no interim dividend shall be paid on shares carrying deferred or non preferred rights if, at the time of payment, any preferential dividend is in arrear. The directors may also pay at intervals settled by them any dividend payable at a fixed rate it it appears to them that the profits available for distribution jutify the payment. Provided the directors act in good faith they shall not incur any liability to the holders of shares conferring preferred rights for any loss they may suffer by the lawful payment of an interim dividend on any shares having deferred or non-preferred rights.

104. Except as otherwise provided by the rights attached to shares, all dividends shall be declared and paid according to the amounts paid up on the shares on which the dividend is paid. All dividends shall be apportioned and paid proportionately to the amounts paid up on the shares during any portion or portions of the period in respect of which the dividend is paid; but, if any share is issued on terms providing that it shall rank for dividend as from a particular date, that share shall rank for dividend accordingly.

105. A general meeting declaring a dividend may, upon the recommendation of the directors, direct that it shall be satisfied wholly or parly by the distribution of assets and, where any difficulty arises in regard to the distribution, the directors may

settle the same and in particular may issue fractional certificates and fix the value for distrituion of any assets and may determine that cash shall be paid to any member upon the footing of the value so fixed in order to adjust the rights of members and may vest any assets in trustees.

106. Any dividend or other moneys payable in respect of a share may be paid by cheque sent by post to the registered address of the person entitled or, if two or more persons are the holders of the share or are jointly entitled to it by reason of the death or bankruptcy of the holder, to the registered address of that one of those persons who is first named in the register of members or to such person and to such address as the person or persons entitled may in writing direct. Every cheque shall be made payable to the order of the person or persons entitled or to such other person as the person or persons entitled may in writing direct and payment of the cheque shall be a good discharge to the company. Any joint holder or other person jointly entitled to a share as aforesaid may give receipts for any dividend or other moneys payable in respect of the share.

107. No dividend or other moneys payable in respect of a share shall bear interest against the company unless otherwise provided by the rights attached to the share.

108. Any dividend which has remained unclaimed for twelve years from the date when it became due for payment shall, if the directors so resolve, be forfeited and cease to remain owing by the company.

ACCOUNTS

(Excluded by Article 1.) 109. No member shall (as such) have any right of inspecting any accounting records or other book or document of the company except as conferred by statute or authorised by the directors or by ordinary resolution of the company.

CAPITALISATION OF PROFITS

110. The directors may with the authority of an ordinary resolution of the company —
    (a) subject as hereinafter provided, resolve to capitalise any undivided profits of the company not required for paying any preferential dividend (whether or not they are available for distribution) or any sum standing to the credit

of the company's share premium account or capital redemption reserve;
(b) appropriate the sum resolved to be capitalised to the members who would have been entitled to it if it were distributed by way of dividend and in the same proportions and apply such sum on their behalf either in or towards paying up the amounts, if any, for the time being unpaid on any shares held by them respectively, or in paying up in full unissued shares or debentures of the company of a nominal amount equal to that sum, and allot the shares or debentures credited as fully paid to those members, or as they may direct, in those proportions, or partly in one way and partly in the other: but the share premium account, the capital redemption reserve, and any profits which are not available for distribution may, for the purposes of this regulation, only be applied in paying up unissued shares to be allotted to members credited as fully paid;
(c) make such provision by the issue of fractional certificates or by payment in cash or otherwise as they determine in the case of shares or debentures becoming distributable under this regulation in fractions; and
(d) authorise any person to enter on behalf of all the members concerned into an agreement with the company providing for the allotment to them respectively, credited as fully paid, of any shares or debentures to which they are entitled upon such capitalisation, any agreement made under such authority being binding on all such members.

NOTICES

111. Any notice to be given to or by any person pursuant to the articles shall be in writing except that a notice calling a meeting of the directors need not be in writing.

112. The company may give any notice to a member either personally or by sending it by post in a prepaid envelope addressed to the member at his registered address or by leaving it at that address. In the case of joint holders of a share, all notices shall be given to the joint holder whose name stands first in the register of members in respect of the joint holding and notice so given shall be sufficient notice to all the joint holders. A member whose registered address is not within the United Kingdom and who gives to the company an address within the United Kingdom at which notices may be given to him shall be entitled to

have notices given to him at that address, but otherwise no such member shall be entitled to receive any notice from the company.

113. A member present, either in person or by proxy, at any meeting of the company or of the holders of any class of shares in the company shall be deemed to have received notice of the meeting and, where requisite, of the purposes for which it was called.

114. Every person who becomes entitled to a share shall be bound by any notice in respect of that share which, before his name is entered in the register of members, has been duly given to a person from whom he derives his title.

115. Proof that an envelope containing a notice was properly addressed, prepaid and posted shall be conclusive evidence that the notice was given. A notice shall be deemed to be given at the expiration of 48 hours after the envelope containing it was posted.

116. A notice may be given by the company to the persons entitled to a share in consequence of the death or bankruptcy of a member by sending or delivering it, in any manner authorised by the articles for the giving of notice to a member, addressed to them by name, or by the title of representatives of the deceased, or trustee of the bankrupt or by any like description at the address, if any, within the United Kingdom supplied for that purpose by the persons claiming to be so entitled. Until such an address has been supplied, a notice may be given in any manner in which it might have been given if the death or bankruptcy had not occurred.

WINDING UP

117. If the company is wound up, the liquidator may, with the sanction of an extrordinary resolution of the company and any other sanction required by the Act, divide among the members in specie the whole or any part of the assets of the company and may, for that purpose, value any assets and determine how the division shall be carried out as between the members or different classes of members. The liquidator may, with the like sanction, vest the whole or any part of the assets in trustees upon such trusts for the benefit of the members as he with the like sanction determines, but no member shall be compelled to accept any assets upon which there is a liability.

INDEMNITY

118. Subject to the provisions of the Act but without prejudice to any indemnity to which a director may otherwise be entitled, every director or other officer or auditor of the company shall be indemnified out of the assets of the company against any liability incurred by him in defending any proceedings, whether civil or criminal, in which judgment is given in his favour or in which he is acquitted or in connection with any application in which relief is granted to him by the court from liability for negligence, default, breach of duty or breach of trust in relation to the affairs of the company.

INDEX

Articles of Association — see Company

Auditor — and see Co-operative Society
   report on purchase by company of its own shares 57

Business expansion scheme 79
Buy-outs
   management 10, 18, 44
   worker 10, 18, 44

Capital
   appreciation 14
   gain, pressure to realise 9, 11, 23, 24, 26, 40
   risk 27
   share 19, 26, 32, 37, 38, 53
Capital contribution
   attitudes 14
   loans or loan stock 27, 43, 103, 128
   Mondragon 25
   partners 31
   profit-sharing scheme 74
   provisions in model 37, 43, 87, 106, 121, 130
   varying with salary 43
   withdrawal 14, 33, 37, 38
Capitalist businesses
   types of 19
Common ownership 27
Company
   accounts 130
   balance sheeet 53
   borrowing
      from members, the prescribed rate 128
   close 63, 77
   control 10, 77
   copy Articles and Table A 131
   directors 32, 35, 47, 57, 71, 77, 125
      appointment 125
      appointment and pensions 126
      contracts in which interested 127
      proceedings of 127
      qualification 125
      quorum 127
      removal 126
      remuneration 126
      voting 127

'employee-controlled' 79
'employee-control shares' 76
family 39, 45
general meetings 124
   notice 124
   proxies 125
   quorum 124
   voting 125
lien 122
limited by guarantee 9, 12, 25
limited by shares ... 10, 31-34, 114, 120
limited liability 19, 32
members 32, 121
   loan accounts 128
   qualification for employee members 121
   reserve accounts 128
memorandum and articles of association
   amendment of 52
   authorised capital 32, 120
   based on Table A 81
   model for worker control .. 12, 13, 52, 55, 60, 62, 76, 114-131
name 114
objects 114
participator 64
pressure to wind up 39, 40
private 120
profits, application of 129
purchase of its own shares 53, 55-57
redemption of shares 45
reduction of capital 33, 53, 56
reserve accounts — and see Reserves 128, 129
share capital 32, 38, 53, 120-122
   cumulative convertible participating preferred ord. shares 46
   employee ordinary shares . 38, 40, 53, 54, 60, 69, 121
   investor shares 81, 122
   ordinary shares 32, 33, 38, 45, 53, 54
   preference shares ... 32, 40, 53, 54, 70
   sale of shares ... 33, 34, 39, 122, 123
   transfer of shares 122, 123
      to employee trust 124
   under control of the directors 120
share redemption reserve

account 40, 41, 45, 53, 55, 56
Table A 120, 147
winding up 32, 39, 131
Contract of Association
   Mondragon 17, 29
Conversion 51-62
   agreement to form worker-
   controlled firm 52, 54
   from worker-control to
   conventional company .. 9, 11, 22,
                                          61, 62
   of company to I & PS Act
   society 57, 58
   of conventional society to worker-
   control 59, 60
   of shares to loan stock ... 37, 58, 59
   purchase of assets and
   goodwill 60, 66
      of existing business 51
      of shares 53
   re-allocation of shares 53-55
   re-organisation of company ... 52,
                                              53
Co-operative
   meaning of 78, 79
   model for workers' control 25,
                                              39
Co-operative Development Agency
(CDA)
   local 9
   national 9, 12
Co-operative Manufacturing
Society 22
Co-operative Productive Federation
(CPF) 22
Co-operative Research Unit (CRU)
   report of conference 13, 16
Co-operative Society
   accounts 110
      annual return to
      Registrar 110
      display of balance sheet ... 110-
                                           111
   advantages 17, 23
   annual general meeting 90
   annual return 110
      supply to interested
      persons 110
   auditor
      access to books 110
      appointment of 108
      attendance at meetings 110
      display of report 110-111
      duties 109
      report 109

      restrictions on
      appointment 108
      return of report to
      Registrar 110
      supply of report 110
   bankruptcy 111
   bona fide 19-21
   bonus payments 105
   books and records 106
      inspection 107
   chairperson
      committee 100
      general meeting 93
   committee 95-101
      appointment 96
      casual vacancies 96
      chairperson 100
      composition 95
      conduct of 100
      co-opted members 96
      disqualification 98
      interest in contract 99
      meetings 100
         notice of 101
      powers and function 95
      quorum 101
      removal 98
      remuneration 98
      retirement 97
      vacancies 97
      voting 101
   conversion — and see Conversion
      of shares to loan stock ... 37, 58
      from company 57
      to company 9, 11, 22, 59, 61
   copies of the rules 107
   death of a member
      cancellation of shares 87
      payment to personal
      representative 111
   decline in number 12, 22, 25
   deposits, prohibition of 89
   discrimination against 17
   dissolution 111
   extraordinary general
   meeting 91
   founder members 75, 84
   funds 90
   indemnity and security of
   officers 107
   inspection of books 107
   interest 11, 20, 26
      loans 89
      reserve accounts 104
      shares 87

investment powers 90
labour hires capital 24, 25
limited liability 19
limited return on capital — see
  "interest" above
loan accounts 103
  interest 103
  repayment 103
meetings
  adjournment of general
    meeting 93
  annual general meeting 90
  committee 100
  conduct of general
    meeting 93
  extraordinary general
    meeting 91
  minutes 103
  notice of committee
    meetings 101
  notice of general meetings .. 91
  proxies 95
  quorum of general
    meeting 92
  quorum of committee
    meeting 101
  rights of auditor 110
  voting at general meeting ... 93
  voting at committee
    meeting 101
members
  control
    by members 11, 20, 24,
                         26, 30
      by employee members . 25,
                     26, 85, 101
        one person one vote 20,
                                   26
  conduct of business for mutual
    benefit 20
  employee and non-
    employee 24
  founder 75, 84
  joint 75
  non-employee 84, 85, 101
  profits according to
    participation 21, 26, 105
  qualification 84
  register of 102
membership 84
  application 86
  restriction 21, 26, 85
  termination 37, 86
name 83
  may not include

'company' 20
nominations of property 111
objects 83
  social 14, 39, 83
officers 102
pensions 84
powers
  borrowing 89
  investment 90
pressure to wind up 24, 26
profit
  application 105
  application of general
    reserve 106
producer, industrial and service
  new wave 25-30
  requirements for worker
    control 25, 26
  traditional 9, 19-25
proxies 95
records and books 106
redemption of shares ... 33, 37, 58,
                          59, 88
register of members 40
registered as a company 25
registered office 84
reserve accounts — and see
  Reserves
  reserve accounts 104
  interest 104, 105
  repayment 104
retail (consumer) 21, 22
rules
  amendment 113
  copies 107
  length 81
  model 9, 12, 13, 26, 58, 59,
                          78, 79
seal 103
secretary
  appointment 102
  duties 102
  keeping of register 106
security and indemnity of
  officers 107
self-exploitation 17
share capital 19, 27, 37, 87
shares 87
  cancellation on death 87
  death of member 111
  interest 87, 105
  maximum holding .. 19, 27, 75,
                               87
  minimum holding 27, 87
  not withdrawable 87

redemption .. 33, 37, 59, 60, 88
transfer 59, 88
termination of membership ... 37, 86
transfer of shares 59, 88
under-capitalisation 17
unprofessional management .. 17
voting
   committee 101
   general meeting 93
winding up ... 9, 12, 14, 27, 39, 112
Co-operative Union 23

Dependants
   beneficiaries of employee
   trust 40, 83, 114, 117, 133, 140
   pension provisions for 39, 73, 84, 117
Directors — see Company
Dissolution — see Winding up

Employee Trust
   dividends taxed 72
   for capitalising reserves ... 40, 132
      beneficiaries 40, 133
      inheritance tax
      considerations 41-43, 132n
      termination 40
      trustees 133
      trustees powers 136
      trusts 40, 134, 135
      vesting day 134
   for gift with tax exemption 63, 139
      beneficiaries 63
      employees' organisation .. 141, 143, 146
      period and terms 66-70
      requirements 63-66
      termination 66, 68, 69
      trustees 140
         control of business 67
         powers 144
         trusts 142, 143
         vesting day 141

Finance
   business expansion scheme 79
   equity shares 43
      a special type 45-47, 54
   financial institutions 44
   greater need for external 47
   guarantees from members 44
   high street banks 44
   ICFC 44, 45
   loans 51, 53, 61
   longer term 44
   security 44
   shares 51, 53, 59, 61
   sources of outside 44

Gift of a company to employees —
and see Employee Trust 63-70

Ideologies 13
Industrial and Commercial Finance
Corporation (ICFC)
   management and worker buy-outs 18, 44
   cumulative convertible
   participating preferred ordinary
   shares 45, 46
Industrial and Provident Societies
Acts (I&PS Acts) 9, 11, 19-24
Industrial Common Ownership
Movement (ICOM) 9, 12, 25, 26-28
   model rules 9, 12, 27, 39
Interest on capital 11, 20, 26

Job Ownership Ltd. (JOL) ... 9, 12, 29, 77
John Lewis Partnership 67

Labour hires capital 24, 25
Loans or loan stock 27, 37, 38, 43, 53, 70
   out of taxed income 72
   postponement to creditors 36n, 38

Management
   accountability 14-16, 47, 48
   Glacier Metal Co. experiment .. 13
   outside the constitution 30
   rotation of function 15
   statutory requirement 14, 47
   structure 47-49
Managers
   accountability 14-16, 47, 48
   fixing salaries of 15
   selecting and dismissing ... 15, 47, 48
Memorandum of Association — see
Company
Members — and see Company and
Co-operative Society
   reserve accounts — see Reserves
   wishes 13, 15, 16, 48
Mondragon Co-operatives 13, 16, 25, 28-30, 36, 43

Objects — and see Company and Co-operative Society
  social 14, 39, 83, 117
Open University Co-operative Research Unit
  report of conference 13, 16

Partnership
  as co-operative 11
    difficulties 30
  as model for co-operative 35
  on purchase of a business by employees 52
  partners binding the firm ... 30, 35
  payment for goodwill on retirement 31
  pensions 31
  reserves 35
  unlimited liability 30, 35
Pay
  differentials 13, 30
  equal 13
Pensions 39, 73
  power to provide in rules 84
  power to provide in articles of association 117
Pension schemes
  exempt approved 73
  partners 31
  pension fund management 73
    investing in the company ... 73
  Privatisation 10
Production
  to meet needs 14
Profits — and see Company and Co-operative Society
  ploughed back .. 23, 24, 26, 27, 33, 36, 47

Profit sharing scheme,
  approved 74-77
    employee-control shares 76
    employee trust 77
    position if our model is used 76
    variations for I&PS Act Societies 74, 75
Promoting body
  contract with co-operatives 17
  providing model constitution .. 17
Proportional representation
  electing board of directors 48, 126n
  electing committee 48, 96n
Purchase of existing business — see Conversion

Proxies — see Company and Co-operative Society

Redundancy Payments 51, 61
Reserves — and see Company and Co-operative Society
  approved profit sharing scheme 74
  building up 27, 33, 34, 36, 39
  capitalising ... 28, 33, 40-43, 58, 73
  destination of 30
  general 36, 39, 40, 53
  members' reserve accounts 36, 58, 72
    repayment of 72
  Mondragon 29
  of purchased company 53
  partnership 31, 35
  provision in models
    articles of association 128, 129, 131
    rules 104, 105, 112
  re-valuation 53, 57
  share redemption reserve account 40, 41, 45, 53, 55, 56
Resource centre
  Mondragon 28, 29
  Trade Union role 16
  Wales TUC 16
Rochdale Pioneers 21
Rules — and see Co-operative Society
  subsidiary 13

Scott Bader Commonwealth 67
Share capital — see Capital, Company and Co-operative Society
Share Premium account 36n

Taxes
  approved profit sharing scheme 74
  business expansion scheme 79
  capital gains tax 63-66
  capital transfer tax — see inheritance tax
  close companies 77
  corporation tax 36, 71-74
    approved profit sharing scheme 74
    exempt approved pension scheme 73
    golden handshakes 72
  exempt approved pension scheme 73

income tax 72
   business expansion
    scheme 79
   golden handshakes 72
   relief for interest on money
    borrowed 77
inheritance tax 41-43, 63-70
on purchase of a business ... 60-61
share of profits taken to loan
   account 72
Trade Unions
   attitude 17
   roles 16
Trustees — see Employee Trust

Wales TUC
   feasibility study 9, 16
   resource centre 9, 16
Widows and dependents
   pension provision .. 39, 73, 84, 117
Winding up
   distribution of surplus assets .. 12,
                 24, 27, 28, 39, 111, 131
Worker buy-outs
   possible growth area 18
Worker control
   generally accepted
    requirements 13, 26
Works Council 48, 68
   John Lewis Partnership 67
   organisation similar to 69